My Progress in Error, and Recovery to Truth
by Unknown

Copyright © 2019 by HardPress

Address:
HardPress
8345 NW 66TH ST #2561
MIAMI FL 33166-2626
USA
Email: info@hardpress.net

Harvard Depository
Brittle Book

Harvard Divinity School

ANDOVER-HARVARD THEOLOGICAL
LIBRARY

MDCCCCX

CAMBRIDGE, MASSACHUSETTS

GIFT FROM
WIDENER LIBRARY

MY PROGRESS IN ERROR,

AND

RECOVERY TO TRUTH.

OR A TOUR THROUGH
UNIVERSALISM, UNITARIANISM,
AND
SKEPTICISM.

BOSTON:
GOULD, KENDALL AND LINCOLN,
59 Washington Street.
1842.

ANDOVER-HARVARD
THEOLOGICAL LIBRARY
CAMBRIDGE, MASS.

H78.416
May 8, 1951

Entered according to Act of Congress, in the year 1841,
By GOULD, KENDALL AND LINCOLN,
in the Clerk's Office of the District Court of Massachusetts.

621
My

WEST BROOKFIELD:
C. A. MIRICK AND CO., PRINTERS.

(Widener)

PREFACE.

Moral and religious error assumes such various shapes, at the present day, especially in this vicinity, as to render it highly desirable that the young should be able to detect it, in all its aspects and windings. Its apostles, too, are as numerous as its forms and shapes; and no men are more active—perhaps I might even say, self-denying. Let the young, then, be put on their guard; and let parents and teachers be guarded on their behalf. To assist parents and teachers, and the youth of our country, in this respect, is the leading object of the following disclosure.

It is not a hasty production. Nearly ten years have passed away since the last of the leading events which it records, transpired. In the mean time, the manuscript has been shown to candid, ingenious, and critical men of most of the principal Christian denominations, and in almost every section of our country. They have unitedly commended it, and requested its publication.

As a specimen of these commendations and requests, I will insert the following note received from an eminent minister of the gospel, who had examined the manuscript with more than ordinary attention.

"Your book, entitled 'My Progress in Error,' &c., I have read with attention and care, and with deep interest. I cannot but think it must prove a useful work to guide the young who are exposed; and one which will be profitable, in many respects, to all classes and descriptions of persons who may read it. I rejoice that you are now, at length, concluding to publish it."

Such flattering notices of my simple story—for I make no claim to a learned production—together with a revival of the Unitarian controversy, and the hope of doing good, have led me to revise the whole, once more, and present it to the Christian public. To that public, and the great Author of Light and Truth, it is now commended, in the hope that it may contribute, in some degree, to hasten the glad day of UNIVERSAL HOLINESS.

THE AUTHOR.

NOVEMBER, 1841.

CONTENTS.

CHAPTER I.

My Education and Early Opinions.—Maternal Influence.—Concientiousness.—Bible in School.—An Infidel visitor in the family.—His life and character.—Became skeptical myself.—Partial conversion.—Franklin for my model.—Hope of being a Philosopher.   9

CHAPTER II.

My Pharisaism.—Life of a Pharisee.—Conviction of sin.—Unitarian Magazine.—Caution to Parents.—An intimate friend.   19

CHAPTER III.

Temporary Reform.—Self-Dedication to God.—Study of certain books.—Imbibed the notion of human perfectibility.—Rejected the doctrine of endless punishment.—My cowardice.—Duplicity.—Effects of error on my moral character.   29

CHAPTER IV.

My progress in Error.—My views of total depravity, &c.—Their obvious absurdity.—Further examples of duplicity.—I became bolder.—Compliments of the "liberal."   41

CONTENTS.

CHAPTER V.

ASSOCIATES IN ERROR.—A Colleague.—Our mutual flattery.—Our first Disciples.—My own morals.—A "liberal Correspondent."—My mode of studying the Bible.—Interest in Sabbath schools.—Formation of a Sabbath school, and a Public Library.—Character of the Books procured. 56

CHAPTER VI.

MY CORRESPONDENTS.—One of my letters.—Various efforts.—Advice of a "liberal" friend.—Conversation.—Education. 67

CHAPTER VII.

ANECDOTES.—Sickness of a young man.—Reflections.—Sickness and death of a disciple in error.—My own "management." 77

CHAPTER VIII.

MY SENTIMENTS ON PRAYER.—External attention to religion.—Specimen of my opinions and mode of reasoning.—Their fallacy shown. 91

CHAPTER IX.

PROGRESS IN ERROR.—My Rationalism.—Interview and discussion with a Minister. 102

CHAPTER X.

MY VIEWS OF REVIVALS, &c.—More facts in regard to my early life. On conscience.—A disputatious turn.—My studies.—Character of my books and associates.—Encouraged by the "liberals." 114

CHAPTER XI.

CHURCH CONFERENCES.—Opposition to these.—One family

with which I was intimate.—Specimens of my manner of talking to them.—The family well nigh ruined. . 126

CHAPTER XII.

My Self-Esteem.—Method of hearing sermons.—Reading books.—Writing a Commentary on the Bible.—An approach to blasphemy.—My creed. 134

CHAPTER XIII.

My Further Progress.—The secret getting out.—How I was treated.—Charges against me.—An injudicious minister.—Word of caution.—Publicly reported that I was a Unitarian.—The consequences. 143

CHAPTER XIV.

My Progress, Continued.—Specimen of my manner of "preaching."—Its effects on Mr. H.—Its general effects.—What was most discouraging about it. 151

CHAPTER XV.

Tour of Observation.—Encouraging circumstances among the Universalists.—Commenced a tour of observation.—Faces of my audiences.—Unitarian preaching and practice.—Meeting with singular individuals.—On the point of going over to the Free Inquirers.—What prevented me.—Re-examined the evidences in favor of a Revelation. 158

CHAPTER XVI.

Speculative Inquiries.—Revelation being admitted, new difficulties arise about some of its doctrines.—The divine nature.—My inquiries.—Dr. Channing's notions of the dignity of human nature.—The views of evangelical sects on this subject. 171

CHAPTER XVII.

My Views in Morals.—Mere morality considered.—Popular mistakes on this subject.—A practical illustration of the difference between morality and religion. 186

CHAPTER XVIII.

My Final Recovery to the Truth.—Stupidity of my mind and heart.—Conviction of danger.—Final resolution.—Change of feeling.—Elements of this change.—Improper encouragement. 193

CHAPTER XIX.

Concluding Remarks.—Present state of the writer.—Appeal to parents.—To the young.—To former disciples.—To associates. 201

Appendix. 219

MY PROGRESS IN ERROR.

CHAPTER I.

EDUCATION AND EARLY OPINIONS.

Maternal Influence.—Conscientiousness.—Bible in School.—
An Infidel Visitor in the family.—His life and character.—
Became skeptical myself.—Partial conversion.—Franklin
for my model.—Hope of being a Philosopher.

THE counsels and guidance of maternal wisdom had so much influence over me during the first years of my existence, that the impressions I received and their tendency to virtuous habits were never in subsequent life wholly eradicated.

Up to the age of ten years, I am not aware that I had ever told a falsehood or used profane language, though both lying and swearing were by no means uncommon in my native neighborhood. My faults, however numerous, were chiefly hid from the public eye. I was esteemed honest, because I was grave; and I was regarded as intelligent, because I could spell, read and write better than other boys of the same age, in the same neighborhood.

My mother's early care had also made me very conscientious. The first falsehood I remember to have told, though I was not detected, cost me many pangs for six or eight months. But my sensibility on this point, gradually wore off.

My Sabbaths were usually spent at church; more, however, as I grew older, in speculating on the character and motives of those around me, and in criticising on the preacher's remarks, than in a useful and profitable manner. Convictions of sin were not unfrequent, but as they usually arose during a time of sickness, or on hearing of some alarming or sudden death, they soon, like the early dew, disappeared.

Having read the New Testament at school till I could almost repeat it, from beginning to end, and having become in some measure disgusted with it,* I seldom read the Bible at all. When I did, it was to find fault with the preacher, or the peculiarities of some sect, or to arm myself with

---

* It was read without explanation or comment; and almost without interest, on the part of either teacher or pupils. It is the *manner* of reading the Bible in schools, and not *the Bible itself*, which produces the effect here alluded to.

weapons for disputation, rather than for the sake of information or improvement.

I had now entered my fourteenth year. At this time, it was my lot often to meet and converse with a very singular individual, by whom my habits, views and feelings were so much modified, and in the end so much injured, that a brief sketch of his character, in this place, will be indispensable.

In his early years, he was industrious, respectable, intelligent and professedly religious. Entering the revolutionary army, as an officer, he gradually became intemperate, as well as addicted to other bad habits. At the close of the war, his feelings having become alienated from his family, he went to a distant state, where he spent more than twenty years.

During all this time he had been drinking deeply of the spirit and sentiments of Thomas Paine, and Ethan Allen, whose characters are well known. He had also become familiar with what has usually been called the "French Philosophy." For the sake of appearances, however, he attached himself sometimes to one sect, and sometimes to another; now to the Episcopalians, and now to the Universalists. Still he remained unreformed.

At length he returned to spend the evening of his days with his former family.

On the decease of his wife, he returned to his old habits of intemperance, and resorted to new connexions, religious and social—virtuous and vicious. Sometimes he seemed to be religious, but at others skeptical—always, however, seeking the friendship of professed Christians with one hand, while he was attempting to destroy the Bible and the religion it inculcates with the other. In one or two instances his partial reformation appeared so hopeful that he was on the point of being admitted to the fellowship of a church. Indeed, in one instance, if I mistake not, he went so far as to submit to baptism.

Notwithstanding all his bad habits, and the constant abuse of his physical frame, he possessed such native strength of constitution that he held out to seventy-nine years of age. He died, as might have been expected, with his bottle at one hand, and his Bible and prayer book at the other.

It was during the last years of his life, that he became a frequent visitor at my father's house. He had read much, and seen a great deal of the world; and he remembered all he had ever heard or known. Much of his conversation was highly

EDUCATION AND EARLY OPINIONS. 13

interesting to me, (anxious as I then was for information,) and might have been useful, had I carefully received the good and rejected the bad.*

To his occasional witticisms, and severe remarks upon Scripture and scripture characters, I was at first as averse as the rest of the family. We soon, however, learned to *endure* them for the sake of peace, as he seemed rather irritable if they were opposed. The more he was indulged, the more bold he grew, and the more strongly he asserted; until for myself, I began to half believe. And had not his wretched moral character disgusted me, I think I should have admitted them still more readily and fully. His ridicule had deceived me, and passed for unanswerable augument.

My skepticism became more and more confirmed till I was sixteen years of age. At seasons, indeed, I experienced convictions of sin, and had the most dismal forebodings of evil; still I could not bring my mind to regard God or futurity as

---

* It is not a little remarkable, that while the old are justly said to "live in the past," and to delight to relate over and over to those that are young, what they have seen and heard, the young, who "live in the future," are equally delighted to hear them; and I cannot help regarding it as a special arrangement of heaven for their early education. But alas! how important is it that these aged instructors of the young should be persons of the right character?

realities. Though I was unwilling boldly to deny, I could not believe. All sacred things appeared to me either visionary or doubtful. "Could I fully believe there is a God," I used often to say to myself, "I would at once prostrate myself before him. If mankind really believe what they profess, how can they be so apparently indifferent? Surely they do not *really believe*. They are as skeptical as myself, but are not so honest as to confess it."

Thus I went on, till I was in my seventeenth year, when a partial change was wrought in my feelings in the following manner. Reading, one day, in the American Preceptor, which was at that time a common school book, I came to this passage; "In the hour of danger and distress, my mind as naturally flies to the Deity for relief, as when hungry I seek food, or when weary, repose."

I was so struck with the truth of this remark, that I admitted at once there must be a God. It is not my intention to say that this consideration is entitled to all the weight, in argument, which I then allowed it;—I am only detailing facts, as they occurred, and influenced my progress.

From this time I became more and more a confirmed Theist, and indeed a partial believer in Revelation. Having been early baptized by an

Episcopal minister, and having been often urged by my godfather and other friends to attend to the rite of confirmation, I at length assented. There was also a confused expectation that some mysterious, unknown, and indescribable change of character and feeling toward God would accompany the rite. I thus became nominally attached to the Episcopal church; though I never ventured to the communion. For a few years after this, I lived the life of a Pharisee; by which is meant that a " form of godliness " was kept up,—though its " power" was unfelt and unknown.

In all my intercourse with mankind, however, I was actuated by the same motives, and governed by the same considerations, as before. In a word, I was *supremely selfish;* and though my friends thought otherwise, conscience and He who implanted it, knew better. The skepticism of the aged individual already alluded to, had made too deep an impression on my youthful mind to be very soon eradicated. It was easy to attend church on the Sabbath, and to pray night and morning—and even to mourn over my departures from duty—but it was not so easy to " go and sin no more."

Many circumstances concurred to render me the victim of my aged friend's seductive influence.

He had made me presents at various times, of various sorts of books. He had put into my hands among other things, a small electrical machine, with the writings of several authors on electricity. Franklin's Moral Philosophy, moreover, was with him a constant theme, and I was gradually led to that attachment to Franklin which better deserved the name of *veneration*, than any feeling which at that time I had towards Him, who is alone the proper object of worship. Franklin somewhere says that he always set a greater value on the character of a "*doer of good*," than on any other kind of reputation—and I early determined to make him my model; and to secure that kind of reputation which he so much valued. Nor is this all. Long before the *external reformation* of which I have spoken took place, the old gentleman said to me one day, gravely and deliberately,—"You must be a *philosopher*." Although I scarcely knew the meaning of the term, yet I knew it meant something which if attained would distinguish me from those around me. I also believed the character of a philosopher to be *attainable*, else why had it been suggested that *I* must become one? As it was something to which Franklin attained, and as he was now to be my model, I had a twofold inducement to press forward for the prize.

For years afterwards, the most pleasing ideas were associated with the word philosopher, whenever I read it, or heard it spoken. Such was my extreme sensibility on the subject, that my face often reddened, and my heart throbbed at the thought of starting out of the ordinary ranks of life, and becoming a philosopher, and *resembling Franklin!* The word *Christian*—and the desire of *becoming* one—or even the name of the Divine *Author* of Christianity, never, in those days, awakened emotions or called up associations half so pleasurable.

It is easy for those who know the laws of the human mind to conceive how perfectly natural it was for me to imbibe, along with this desire for distinction so early implanted by my aged friend, much of his skepticism; and how tenaciously I should be apt to retain it. And these facts are mentioned to show the danger of permitting youth to associate with such men—however wise or amiable. The moral character may, in this way, be insensibly poisoned; and the evil may be, as it probably will be, in the present instance, as lasting as life itself.

That "each bitter has its sweet," is not to be denied. *That ambition* which now pervaded my whole soul, stimulated me to make progress in many things, where I should probably have remained stationary without it. It also kept me from grovelling in some of those depths of vice to which I was peculiarly exposed by the state of the society in which I moved; and it led me to make several praiseworthy efforts for the moral and intellectual improvement of the youth around me. These efforts, it is true, for want of the support of my fellow youth, were unsuccessful; but they served to stamp the character.

While, however, the ambition to become great and distinguished operated as a restraint, in some respects, it tended to set me free in others. I made (*practically* I mean,) all virtue to consist in securing the approbation of the wise and good; but whatever vice I believed to be concealed and likely to remain concealed from the public eye, there was nothing to shield me from committing.

CHAPTER II.

MY PHARISAISM.

Life of a Pharisee.—Conviction of sin.—Unitarian Magazine.—Caution to Parents.—An intimate friend.

I HAVE said in the preceding chapter that I became a Pharisee. My pharisaic course continued till I was more than twenty years of age. During a part of this time, I had the care of youth; and how many souls I ruined, it is impossible for me to say. They witnessed my external compliance with some of the *forms* of religion, it is true; but their scrutinizing eyes could not have failed to discover that my *heart* was unaffected by it. I shudder, almost, when I think what may have been the result of my influence.

But it pleased Him who has in his hands the hearts of all men, occasionally to make me tremble in view of my impenitence and sin. Dissatisfied with myself and the world, I smothered, or attempted to smother my dissatisfaction, by visiting new regions, seeing new faces, and engaging in new employments. I spent some time at a distance from my former associates. But the sickness and death of near relatives and friends recalled me, at length, to myself, though it produced a state of mind scarcely more favorable than skepticism. For a long time I was so disgusted with myself and with the world, that I shunned as much as possible, all society; and even refused to attend church on the Sabbath: regarding it as only adding to my guilt, and hardening me against every religious impression. In company, I was completely miserable; in solitude scarcely less so. In a word, I abandoned myself to misanthropy.

However, as the result of causes which cannot here be given in detail, this state of feeling gradually wore off, and my mind became more composed and cheerful. Resolutions of amendment and of a religious life, were now occasionally made and broken; and though I had some time before abandoned the forms of religion and regarded myself as 'without God in the world,' I yet lived for a time on these resolutions. This, if no better, was at least no worse than the horrors of misanthropy.

On the subject of religion, I was all this while laboring under one unhappy error. Some sort of interference of a supernatural character in which I was to be wholly passive like a mere machine, and in which I had no concern nor agency whatever, was supposed to be indispensable before I could be prepared even to attempt a new and holy life. It was an interference, of a kind, too, in which—though not quite a miracle—my moral and intellectual faculties were supposed to have nothing to do.

I am sorry to say that I cannot help believing views of this kind to be very common; and I wish Christian ministers would labor and pray more earnestly on this very point. I am far from admitting, with the enemies of evangelical religion, that such views have their origin in Calvinism, or indeed in any *particular* form of Christian belief. They are only a species of fatalism most prevalent where the gospel light never shone; and which, where it has shone, it has not yet been able fully to dislodge.

About this period of my life, a religious excitement prevailed where I was residing. After opposing it for some time and endeavoring to show its unreasonableness, I altered my purpose, and resolved to attend meetings regularly, in the hope that some "mercy drops" from the passing cloud, if it really contained any, might fall on me. And toward the close of the excitement I began to believe my heart had been touched;—though my friends always seemed to have more charity for me than I ever had for myself.

This at least is true, the forms of a religious life were once more resumed, and for a few years, the reformation seemed to be something more than merely an external one. For my own part, doubts of my real conversion were so strong, that they prevented me from becoming attached to any church, although I became a teacher in Sunday schools, and a regular and outwardly devout attendant on religious worship.

It was at this period of my life that I first fell in with a Unitarian Magazine. It contained an account of the conversion of an orthodox minister to Unitarianism. Till this hour I scarcely knew there was such a thing as a Unitarian in the United States.

I read this pamphlet with precisely those prejudices which almost every one indulges who has been allowed, and even *trained* to believe that every sect or class of individuals is wholly wrong but his own; and that the religion of his fathers must necessarily be true. A Unitarian, above all, I regarded as a kind of monster in human shape. Indeed, I cannot say that I ever felt more curiosity to see monsters, in nature, than I did, after reading this pamphlet, to see some individual belonging to that sect. Of course, in taking a book containing their views into my hand, I was gratifying in a degree, this curiosity; mingled, however, with a species of horror, very unfavorable to a careful appreciation of the subject.

And here I must be permitted to solicit parents, should any such ever take the trouble to read these remarks, to prevent, by all possible means, these unreasonable prejudices from taking root in the minds of their children; for they will either be likely to make them bigoted, or what is scarcely worse, to lead them, whenever they come to examine, to examine superficially, and ultimately to go to the other extreme—I mean, to skepticism.

Those who differ from us on the subject of religion should be still regarded as men; and commiserated, rather than despised for their opinions, however heterodox, they may appear. The former feeling in a parent, will rarely, if ever, mislead a child,—the latter may be construed in a species of persecution. Now children possess too much of that common nature in which we all participate, not to sympathize with the persecuted. Or should they escape this danger, that curiosity may be awakened which will lead, as in my own case, to an imperfect and partial investigation, and ultimately to downright error.

No person is more exposed to skepticism—or rather to vibrate from one extreme to another—than he who is trained a bigot ; however ignorant many parents and teachers appear to be of this fact. Perhaps there is no sect in the world whose adherents approach nearer the borders of downright skepticism, than the *superficially* enlightened among the bigoted Catholics of France, and the other old countries.

Above all, and while I think of it, let me solicit parents and those who have the care of children, not to *conceal* from a child any book, as improper for him, which the child has reason to think the parents, themselves, are fond of perusing. I have known much mischief produced in this way. Nay, I think immortal souls have been ruined—eternally so—by this injudicious management. Better, by far, as it appears to me, that the worst books should be within reach of a child, than that he should detect a parent in attempts to conceal them.

But to return from this digression. I rose from the perusal of the pamphlet above mentioned to *condemn*, but not to *forget* it. I had read it as if by stealth, and I distinctly remember that in regard to its perusal I had some of the feelings with which they are tormented who have actually committed an offence against the law of God or the land.

Not long afterward, while conversing with an intimate friend, whom I knew to have considerable knowledge of the Scriptures, I ventured to ask, whether we were required, in the New Testament, to pray to Christ; and whether it could be shown that the apostles or any of the first Christians *ever did* pray to him. She replied that there were accounts of the kind, but she could not tell where. I begged her to point out only a single instance. This she was unable, at the time, to do! And although I did not choose to protract the conversation for fear of being regarded as inclining to error, yet I could not forbear feeling as if I had achieved a victory. So common is it to construe the silence of an opponent, or his inability to defend his views, into a weakness of the cause he is advocating. Yet what can be more unreasonable!

I might have been told that there was no occasion for prayer to the Savior while he was on earth, but that in almost every *recorded* prayer, made by the apostles and Christians after his death, where the *object is mentioned*, and in almost every account of such prayers, whether made individually or collectively, it is clearly evident that they were directed to Christ. Indeed the question might almost be asked; when was prayer (as recorded in the Bible) made in any other manner?

The first prayer after Christ's death, whose form is recorded, was that which was made at the selection of an apostle to supply the place of Judas. The language was; "Thou, Lord, which knowest the hearts of all men, show whether of these two thou hast chosen." Did not Jesus choose all the rest? And is it not perfectly clear that it was he to whom the appeal was *now* made? For one, I have not a doubt on the subject.

In the next instance, Acts, 4 : 24, prayer seems, indeed, to have been directed to the Father. The next two cases in point are the two prayers of Stephen, both of which were evidently to Christ. The next two, or three,—if indeed they may be called prayers—were by Saul and Ananias—and were also addressed to the Savior. Acts, 12 : 5, and 21 : 25, are more doubtful.

In the Epistles, however, mention is made of "calling" upon Christ, which of course is nothing less than prayer. Again, James seems to refer to prayer to Christ, when he says that in answer to the prayer of faith for the sick, "the Lord shall raise him up." And if these instances had not been sufficient, I might have been quoted to several passages in the Revelation, which, if they have any meaning at all, confirm the same point. But these had escaped the notice or memory of my friend, as well as myself; though perfectly *obvious* to every common sense reader of the New-Testament who is unprejudiced.

No further opportunities of perusing Unitarian publications occurred for sometime. My doubts became in some measure quieted, though I was not perfectly satisfied. But my religious impressions gradually wore off; and this result was greatly forwarded by associating with a gentleman of strong powers of mind, and enlarged and liberal sentiments, but so violent against cant and hypocrisy as to indulge occasionally in sneers and insinuations against all public professions of religion; and in appearance, against religion itself.

During this time I was a firm supporter of Sabbath schools, and of all measures for the promotion of learning and religion. A strong attachment to Masonic institutions had the effect, however, to alienate my mind from the subject of religion; although I do not affirm that this is, always, a necessary result of those institutions: I only speak of their effect on myself. Public worship I attended regularly, and I began to think it was quite possible to be a Christian without being attached to a church, or even to a sect; and gradually fell into the belief that it was my duty to stand aloof from what I regarded as narrow sectarian schemes and measures. Like thousands of others, I neglected the appointed means of growth in grace, under the specious plea that it was better to make no pretensions at all to religion, than to *profess*, and yet not govern myself accordingly.

CHAPTER III.

TEMPORARY REFORM.

Self-Dedication to God.—Study of certain books.—Imbibed the notion of human perfectibility.—Rejected the doctrine of endless punishment.—My cowardice.—Duplicity.—Effects of error on my moral character.

MONTHS and years passed away, and with them the fervor of that confidence in God which I had been accustomed to cherish. I found myself relapsing into the habit of regarding both public and private worship as matters of form merely—praying and praising, and hearing, as though I *prayed, and praised, and heard not*—and of indulging myself to the full extent in speculating on the preacher—his style, manner, doctrine, motives;—and the motives, manners, and character of the hearers. In a word, I became habituated to seeing "all other's faults," without feeling "my own."

But in the midst of this career, I was suddenly arrested;—I can hardly tell how. The lowering heavens seemed to gather blackness around me, and in the midst of gloom mixed with terror, I was providentially directed to the famous work of Dr. Doddridge, entitled, the "Rise and Progress of Religion in the Soul." I read it with avidity, and it inspired me with new hopes. It made me feel that I was not yet lost, but that something could be done. Still I am not aware that it led me to feel, in any great degree, my utter helplessness, without divine aid. On the contrary, I am not certain but I was inclined, from this time, to trust more strongly in an 'arm of flesh,' than ever.

But from repeated perusal of Dr. Doddridge's "Examples of Self-Dedication," or "Solemn form of renewing our covenant with God," I was at last led to regard it as my *own* duty to attempt something of the kind. A day and spot were fixed upon; pen, ink, and a form were prepared, and nothing remained but to affix my name to the instrument.

The day appointed was the Sabbath; the spot a sequestered bluff, overlooking, at a distance, a humble parish church, surrounded by a few farmers' houses; the precise hour, the setting of the sun. And what rendered the romance, (for there was much of romance blended with the rest,) still more romantic, it was one of the most beautiful October evenings, which the world ever beheld.

With my paper, ink, &c., before me, I was at the spot, seeking, as I believed, divine aid in my undertaking, during the last hour of the sun,—at the termination of which, I solemnly affixed my name to the "instrument."

In this instrument I had taken so much pains to guard against future heresy, that I verily think the measure tended to defeat one of the purposes for which it was made. The language was very strong. The pledge to invoke Father, Son, and Spirit, in every instance of morning and evening worship as long as I should live, had a very sinuglar effect. It produced a re-action. That this would have been the result on other minds is not certain; but in my own case, with the "ghosts of departed" *skepticism* hovering about me, this was the undoubted effect. It led me to reflect on my failures, and at the same time, *almost always*, to investigate the doctrine which it involved. And at length when by accident or forgetfulness the pledge *was violated, it led me, as it were, to wish*, secretly, I hardly know why, that the doctrine of the Trinity were not well substantiated. Thus does man, feeble as he is, vainly attempt to lower the demands of his Creator; and, to avoid punishment, works himself into the belief that he has committed no crime! For, "what ardently we wish, we soon believe."

During all this time, I was much employed, in various ways, in attempting to improve the condition of the young. In directing my attention to those means and facilities for effecting my purposes, which lay within my reach, several very interesting works on education fell in my way, and among others, some of the French writers, on Physiology, such as Magendie and Richerand. The moral views of these writers, so far as they can be inferred from physical doctrines, were borrowed from Kant and other writers of the same school; and though I little understood either the one or the other, yet I flattered myself I knew how to appreciate both. The only periodical in this country, which was devoted to the subject of education, and which had just at this time made its appearance, favored as I thought the same views; and whatever may have been the real intention of the writer, many doctrines there advanced, seemed to me to inculcate such views of primal purity and innocence, and of the possible perfection of humanity in individuals, as well as in the mass of society, as were at variance with evangelical religious sentiments.

To the observer of human nature, such as it is, (whether viewed in the light of common sense or Revelation,) it is almost unnecessary to say which way my speculative mind inclined.

The existence of no object under the full blaze of a meridian sun appeared to me more clearly established than the "perfectibility" of human nature, could we subject that nature from the earliest moments to appropriate influences. From the perfectibility of the infantile individual, I proceeded by easy marches to that of the whole race of infants; from that of infants to that of adults in some golden period of the world, (and at my age, and with such views, the *golden* age would of course be set in the future,) when schools and churches, and alms houses, and prisons, and penitentiaries should become what they ought to be—places of moral and physical reformation, and not of increasing preparation for destruction. From the doctrine of perfectibility on earth, I proceeded at length to that of general or universal perfection beyond the grave. "What shall we think," I used to say, "of the Governor of worlds infinite, who cannot carry the reforming process infinitely farther than the petty governors of a world like this?" "Stand by now, ye sage proclaimers of the doctrine of endless punishment," thought I, "for I am a little wiser, if not 'holier,' than to believe your dogmas."

It was forgotten that every plan for human improvement, comes too late for the generation of *six thousand years that are gone by;* and that supposing God's ways are as our ways, and His thoughts as our thoughts, and that the power of human perfectibility were even to be attained at some future period, and a long millennium of three hundred and sixty-five thousand years should dawn on this darkened world, there would still remain a portion of our race—numerous almost, as the millions from Adam to this hour—who are gone beyond the "bounds of time and space," without undergoing the "reforming process;" and entered on a world where no "sure word of prophecy," whatever may be our *speculations*, guarantees any change.

The arguments derived from Scripture in favor of "final restoration," are specious, I know; but they are certainly unsound. But I have no time to examine them in this place. Nor is it at all necessary, as they are believed to have been often fairly met and fairly answered. I will only add, that the plain, common sense language of the Bible, imperfect as some parts of the translation may possibly be, would never, in my view, lead a person to Universalism, until he *had* first felt the inconvenience of the commonly received doctrine, or until speculative studies had rendered him the victim of a degree of mental hallucination. It is even said by a considerable portion of the Germans, (who are highly speculative,) according to Mr. Dwight, that they reject the doctrine of future endless punishment, rather because *they conceive it to be* derogatory to the character of God, than because they do not find it revealed in the Scriptures.

To *me*, however, its *effect* is no small evidence of its unsoundness. And first its effect on my own mind and heart. After the *light*, as I called it, began to break in upon me, it gave a new impulse to my feelings, as well as to my whole character. The freedom from those narrow sectarian notions in which I had been educated, the pleasure I anticipated in braving the storm of public opinion, when it should be no longer possible to conceal the change of sentiment,—but above all, the satisfaction of being a little wiser and better than the "common herd" of my fellow men, and standing out of their ranks in "full relief;" these considerations, I say, had great weight on my mind. Mine was a lofty eminence; mankind were among the hills and dales below;—mine was a "Goshen," where the sun of science and morality shone with its best beams;—theirs Egyptian darkness and superstition ! ! ! "Poor fellow men," I used to exclaim, in imagination," how much are you to be pitied !"

If we look a little farther, perhaps we shall find

how great a measure of pity was really demanded. As might have been expected, I spared no pains in endeavoring to convert my friends and neighbors to the true "faith," as I regarded it; though in general, rather by the Socratic mode of argument, and by throwing difficulties in the way of their former belief, than by openly avowing, and boldly and honestly inculcating my own sentiments; not without exciting suspicion, however, of what for some time could not be proved. But one day in conversation with a person, I incautiously told him that, "if I thought the Bible *contained* the doctrine of endless future punishment, I would not believe it."

Now the secret was out. The man reported that I had declared myself a Universalist. The people stared, and a few believed. And, reader, what course do you suppose I took? I boldly *denied* the fact, and said the gentleman misunderstood me; thus sheltering myself from public odium by a falsehood, and what was still worse, by throwing the lie upon my unoffending friend and neighbor. What could have been more base! Who was the real object of "pity" now? Yet such is the *cowardice*, as well as the baseness of error! Such the depth of degradation to which I fell!

It may be said that though the views which I had embraced *might*, in this single instance, have led to such results as have been described, yet it does not follow that such would be the *general* consequence. This is admitted. Yet so far as I have observed, and am able to judge from many years acquaintance with the world, it is my *opinion* that such is generally the case. That many persons who embrace the sentiments in question are moral men, is undoubtedly true ; but is the world indebted to their peculiar views for this morality ? They were not generally educated in them. Their habits were very often formed under evangelical sentiments. They ate and drank the milk of "orthodoxy."—By her maternal influences, by her schools, and by her churches, their characters became what they are. Habit is second nature. And second nature is usually as strong—sometimes stronger—than *first* nature. Until Universalism has been handed down through several generations of individuals and collective bodies, is it not premature to say, that the same habits and character which are proved by centuries to be the result of evangelical sentiments, do not *originate* in this very source when found in those (or their parents,) who were educated in them ?

"By their fruits ye shall know them," it is true; but which are the legitimate fruits of evangelical sentiments, and which those of *other* sentiments in the case of persons born and nurtured in the former? A *family* or even a *church*, of a century's standing, when surrounded by a multitude of other families and churches of different sentiments, cannot exhibit its distinctive tendency or character. The character of its most zealous adherents, will be greatly modified—perhaps even more affected—by the character of *society in general*, than by that of a single family or church embracing *different* views. Is it too much to say that the *real fruits* of many of our minor sects in this country —and especially of the Universalists, and Unitarians, has not yet been tested—and whether they are very good, after all, cannot yet be fully ascertained?

I have said that the fact of a man's sustaining a good moral character *to-day*, is not positive proof that it is the result of the *principles he now holds.* But when a person who was bred to good habits, becomes suddenly depraved, after embracing new sentiments, there is reason to *suspect*, at least, the tendency of those sentiments. The evidence in the case is increased, in proportion to the number of persons embracing them, and pursuing a similar vicious course, and the absence of other causes adequate to the production of the supposed change of character.

In my own case, there were many causes to prevent new principles, however erroneous, from producing *immediate* evil results.——Owing to my uncommon gravity, and certain traits of character which had existed from my earliest years, public opinion had been enlisted, in an unusual degree in my favor. I had been, during every period of my life, highly flattered; and, to some extent, at least, respected. While a mere lad, I had been employed a part of the time, for years, to read the sermons in a small society of Episcopalians who were destitute of a minister; and I was scarcely twenty years of age when I occasionally read the Liturgy——a task usually assigned to people somewhat advanced in life——especially those who are of the laity. These facts are mentioned in order to show that I had a character to sustain by good behavior, or jeopardize by misconduct. Yet in spite of all this we see to what a slight temptation——comparatively so, I mean, I yielded.

There is another fact which increases the probability that loose principles led to loose morality in my own case: I allude to the fact that my new principles gave for a time——as has already been observed——a new impulse to my feelings ; and led me to estimate myself much higher than before. Now it is well known that, other things being equal, the higher our self-respect, the more likely we are to withstand temptation.

CHAPTER IV.

MY PROGRESS IN ERROR.

My views of total depravity &c.—Their obvious absurdity—Further examples of duplicity—I became bolder—Compliments of the "liberal."

My belief in infantile purity excluded also the doctrine of total depravity. Indeed this last had been given up earlier than the doctrine of eternal punishment. Perhaps I shall be unable to express my views, at this time, in a better manner than by introducing a paragraph or two from some remarks on education, written about that time, which I still carefully preserve as a relic of what I once was. The reader will see how nearly they correspond with the views of some of our new-light men of 1840, and 1841. Besides, they give the best possible account of my progress at this period. The first paragraph is as follows :—

"The noble prerogative of being mothers, involves a high and heavenly trust. Receiving the infant being from the hands of a holy God, they are to preserve it *uncontaminated* from the world. They have in charge the crystal fountain, *before its waters are rendered impure* by the stagnated and sickly streams of a depraved world.—They are to guard the avenues to vice, by preserving the rectitude of the senses ;—by eliciting the affections, and directing them to their appropriate objects :—and in a word, by forming holy and heavenly character. A noble prerogative truly ;—that of guiding, as the appointed instruments,—God's noblest work into two worlds, earth and heaven !"

It is obvious that the doctrine of " native innocence and purity" is here recognized ; and that the doctrine of evangelical Christians, that a *special Divine influence*, is requisite, along with our own efforts, in order to secure salvation—however plainly taught in the Bible, is rejected.

The next paragraph alluded to, is much longer ; and is a strange medley of truth and error.

" Man is, indeed, in every instance, farther below the Deity in point of perfection than it is either his interest or his duty to be ; and farther off from what the perfection of God's law requires than he would have been if he had properly improved his talents. In this sense, ' there is none righteous, no, not one ;' there is no person so near God as he might be. Every thought, feeling, action or word, which is less pure, or less perfect, than it might have been, is sinful. *All* is sin, in this point of view; and mankind are, if you please, in this respect, totally depraved. And the time probably never will come when a single individual of the human race will be any other than totally depraved, in the sense here explained, unless that individual shall become equal to the Deity. For the human soul, considered in its relation to the Creator, is justly said by Addison to be like one of those mathematical lines which may approach each other to all eternity without the possibility of touching.

" Still I believe that multitudes of the human race do feel, think, speak and act in some degree correctly: that is, in such a manner, that God is better pleased with it than if the manner were different; therefore they are *not* totally depraved. Those human beings whose depravity has sunk them the lowest, do, in some instances, perform actions which evince that there is a spark of a Divine or spiritual nature latent within them,— smothered, indeed, and almost extinguished,— but ready to break forth, and burn brighter and brighter 'unto the perfect day,' when the present barbarous theology shall give place to one which in the language of a vulgar maxim, will give even the devil his due, and man the little portion of credit which is justly due him.

"While, therefore, I am a believer in human depravity to as great an extent as any person has ever conceived it to exist, I also believe in human excellence. Go where you will among the numerous varieties of the human race, and you will find excellent traits of character,—oftener indeed among the European race of men, which has been most under the influence of Christianity—but even among the most barbarous of our species. To the truth of these statements the travels of Park, Mackenzie, Ledyard, and a thousand other credible men will amply attest.

"History—*profane* history at least—is scarcely any thing more than a record of human crimes and follies. Were we to judge of human nature by these alone, no wonder if we came to the conclusion that man is totally depraved. But no history has ever been written which does justice to the human character. The thousand and ten thousand times ten thousand acts of kindness which have been performed in the exercise of the social affections ;—the happiness which has been diffused through the domestic circle by parents, children, husbands, wives, brothers, sisters, &c.—has never had a historian since time began. This record is *on high* alone, and will testify that the God within the human being has had an influence to remove human misery,—the soulless doctrine of human depravity to the contrary notwithstanding.

" It is to no purpose to urge that the motives which dictate the common virtues of mankind are purely selfish ; for what motives but selfish ones influence the most exalted saint on earth? That a good man regards the happiness of his *nobler* nature, as well as the joys of his *animal* existence, I admit, but still he is selfish. Strictly speaking, no such thing as disinterested benevolence can be found. Will it be said that the saint *forgets* self, and acts solely with a view to the glory of God ? But why should he seek to promote God's glory ? Simply because the employement gives him exalted pleasure ;—adds to his mental and moral happiness.

"If human vice be adduced in proof of depravity, human virtue should be admitted in proof of human holiness. The truth is, mankind are both depraved and holy ;—mixed characters.

" Suppose the multitude of kind words and actions which have rendered the social and domestic circle scenes of comparative happiness, and made human society on the whole tolerable, had never existed ; and that their place had been filled by malicious words and conduct ;—suppose, in one word, that no virtue of any kind had ever existed in the world ;—how different would have been our condition ! Then we might, in truth have talked of total depravity.—But the case is far otherwise. There is *goodness* in the world. Human beings are the authors of that goodness. And the authors of goodness are not totally depraved.

" This disheartening doctrine has, however, found its way into the world, and sunk the human mind lower than it otherwise would have been. Partly believing themselves to be totally destitute of any likeness to the Deity, mankind have gradually approximated *toward* that condition. They have become the slaves of fear ; and fear is a depressing passion. Accustomed to hear religious instructors forever declaiming against depravity, they have acquired a habit of looking too much on the dark side of things. A moral hypochondria prevails throughout the religious world ; although a few individuals may have escaped its influence. And *moral* hypochondria produces the same species of *physical* disease. Our hopes of heaven and happiness are more rarely appealed to. Death and hell are continually set forth in all their horrors, both real and imaginary, and the fear of those is considered a proper and legitimate motive to present to rational and immortal agents. People who are accustomed to turn their attention to the dark side of things, will never, either in a physical or moral point of view, be in health.

"No wonder, then, at the prevalence, both of physical and moral hypochondria! The wonder is that mankind are ever brought from darkness to light,—from the habit of looking downward to that of looking heavenward."

The strange absurdities, and glaring contradictions, not to say downright atheism of this long extract, will probably disgust some of my readers. But strange and inconsistent as it may appear, it is just such reasoning as passes very current with a certain portion of society. I have stood by the intemperate, the gluttonous, and the debauched, and seen their hollow eyes brighten at the *glad tidings* that there are no persons without a "spark of the divine nature" within them, however vicious ; that the more exalted christians differ from other men only in having more of the "divine nature," and less of selfishness in them than others ; and that the highest saint is only and entirely "selfish." I have seen the covetous and the extortioner remit, for a moment, their efforts to "devour widows' houses" and " grind the faces of the poor," to hear from a man whose moral character, externally, was unimpeachable, and who was supposed to be qualified to testify from his own experience in regard to the nature of Christian views, feelings and motives. How did they feel encouraged to prosecute their accursed purposes under the specious plea that they were doing no more than the best of men were accustomed to do ; viz., promote in the greatest possible degree their self-interest !

Yes, I have again and again seen men give themselves over to every evil work under the debasing influences of views like the foregoing ; and I have been confounded too at the result, for I thought that by removing from their minds the antiquated and erroneous notion of " total depravity," the " fear of hell," and other "narrow" and "gloomy" theological notions, I should exalt them into a happier region, and a purer atmosphere of moral feeling, such as that to which I fancied I had attained.

The *contradictions* of the above views were not perceived at the time, even by myself. The absurdity of claiming a portion of the " divine nature" for those whose principles almost exclude God, was forgotten. If the highest standard of human action be a regard to our own temporal and eternal good, of what purpose is any *higher* standard or law? Should it be said that promoting our "own glory" promotes the "glory of God" at the same time, the reply is; of what consequence then, is it to *have* any regard for the glory of God? All that men have to do, at this rate, is to promote their own happiness, in a physical, moral, and intellectual point of view. What is wanted is only to enlighten mankind on this subject, and to train the rising generation according to this "new light," and the work of human regeneration is completed. Then, at least, God may be set aside as of no further use. The highest human wisdom will be to become what in fact we shall then find ourselves,—practical atheists.

In truth, throughout the whole of the above tissue of error, the doctrine of human depravity, as held by evangelical christians, and as it is believed to be set forth in the Bible, is utterly misrepresented. No intelligent man has ever pretended to deny the existence of moral virtues domestic, social and public. These have often abounded, and have greatly improved the otherwise dreary aspect of the world. But even these are unquestionably the results of that religion, operating on the mass of society through the medium of its institutions, whose doctrines include the one in question. Total depravity is an absence of the fear and love of God. Men may perform many actions, which are right in themselves, without so much as caring whether or not there is a God in the universe. Surely these acts can have nothing to do with holiness; for otherwise that kind of honor which prevails amongst the most lawless banditti, and without which their clan could not be kept together, would be holiness. He who will not plunge his dagger in a fellow being merely because he has eaten salt with him, though he butcher a dozen persons the next hour, is, at this rate, so far as his regard to this point if honor is concerned, a holy person, a child of God. But this cannot be, of course.

"To the law and to the testimony." If we admit that there be law and testimony, the question after all, is, What do they affirm? It is not so much what *we think* would be fit and proper, as what God has said *is* and *shall be.* The law and the testimony are *plain* and consistent in all essential points and facts, so that the "wayfaring men, though fools, shall not err therein."

But my views of depravity were greatly confirmed by the conclusion that " mankind universally tend to become what they are taken to be."

"If we take them to *mean* well," said I—" to res*pect themselves,* and *to desire improvement in knowledge and virtue,* they will naturally come to possess these views, feelings and intentions. If, on the other hand we take them to be the contrary of all this, their respect for themselves will gradually diminish, and their progress will be downward." It was hence fully believed that the doctrine of man's utter destitution of real holiness by nature, so generally taught, had the effect to debase the human character. "Christ himself," I used to say, never "taught the doctrine of total depravity," for the *common people heard him gladly,—the world went after him, &c.* And how could this have happened if he had denounced them all as sinners indiscriminately? No; it was the chief priests, and the mischief making ringleaders of the Jews alone, on whom fell the dreadful denunciation ; *ye serpents, ye generation of vipers, &c.*

Contradictory and unscriptural as most of these views were, to many they appeared specious, and to some, rational. The more I promulgated them, and especially with success, the more I was confirmed in them. Many things which I at first threw out as much to startle people by their novelty, as for any other purpose, became at length as firmly fixed as any other articles of my creed. I remember one circumstance of this kind in particular. In maintaining that to *take* mankind to be sinful, or capable of sin, was a sure way to *make* them so, it was argued that on this principle the Creator's prohibition to our first parents had a tendency to bring about their fall. This, I maintained, did not necessarily follow. Still, I knew upon reflection that it did; and to evade the consequences, I began to maintain that the story of the fall was a mere allegory. And though this opinion was thrown out merely to serve my purpose at that particular moment, it was not long before I fully adopted it.

Experience keeps a dear school, but there are those who will learn in no other. By an experience, the most painful, I have at length learned as I have before intimated, how dangerous is the practice—to ourselves, if not to others—of advancing opinions which we do not fully believe; for having in this way publicly adopted them, we seem to act on the principle that we are pledged to support and defend them; and in searching for auguments for this purpose, we gradually lose sight of the strength of those on the other side of the question. Let me warn my readers, especially young men, as they value their own present and eternal peace, entirely to avoid this error. It is one of the rocks on which very many split.

The maxim that taking mankind to be bad tends to make them so, might be more nearly correct, if no hope of improvement were held out to them. But generally there is. All laws, human and divine, which proclaim the penalties of transgression, *imply*, if they do not *express*, the power of avoiding the crime, and consequently its penalty. But this supposes a bright as well as a dark side of the picture. The subjects of the law are taken to be *good*, as well as *bad*; or rather they are taken to be *capable* of goodness, if they seek the appropriate means and aid. It is indeed true that the " common people heard " Christ, " gladly," but it is also true that he taught,—and clearly too—that they were by nature destitute of holiness. The command to *repent*, was to *all*, or it had *no* meaning. All were commanded to repent, for without repentance, all were explicitly said to be in danger of perishing. But this was certainly taking them all to be more or less vile, else what need was there of repentance? Indeed, the depravity of man is so well known, and *felt* too, by every rational individual, that any measures for human improvement which do not take this doctrine as their basis, would be retarded, from the very fact, that there was a suppression of the truth.

" By this time I was fully prepared to inculcate

new views on every convenient occasion. My employment was of such a nature as to give me leisure and the means of access to many individuals who were prepared to hear me inculcate any doctrines whose tendency was to lower the terms of the gospel. I found a little difficulty, it is true, with the reports that were circulated of my heresy. But I gradually fell into a habit of evading them, by saying that I was misunderstood; or by a species of duplicity which I sometimes practiced.—For when asked by the friends of evangelical views, if I rejected certain of their doctrines, I usually replied in the negative; reserving to myself always the right of using and explaining terms in a manner entirely different from that to which I knew they were accustomed—a practice which certainly cannot be justified.

In this way I went on for some time. When in the company of the friends of orthodox religious views, I avowed a belief in depravity, the eternity of future punishment, &c. When with others, I evaded, and sometimes denied and ridiculed them. It is surprising that my character for truth and integrity did not suffer more than it did; and to me still more surprising that I should have been influential in creating so strong a prejudice in the minds of many against those doctrines in which they had been educated—a prejudice which probably no efforts of my own can ever fully remove.

And at this stage of my progress, with how much complacency did I view my own character and attainments! Naturally diffident, modest, unassuming, I became occasionally, in conversation, bold, positive, overbearing, and sometimes censorious. By my own estimate, all mankind but myself and a few *other* "thinking men," of "liberal views," were "ignorant," "illiberal," "uncharitable," "prejudiced," "bigoted," "narrow," "contracted," &c. Indeed there were no epithets which I did not apply to the multitude of my fellow men, when in the company of those whom I thought would tolerate it. Of this class, it is true, I found but a small number, but they were "choice spirits." I had also a few "choice" correspondents, who did all in their power to encourage "free inquiry," and "liberal and original thinking." I was complimented both directly and indirectly, as a "light shining in a dark place," destined ultimately to scatter the rays of truth over a great moral and intellectual waste. I was yet to make the "wilderness and the solitary place glad, and the desert rejoice and blossom as the rose."

CHAPTER V.

ASSOCIATES IN ERROR.

A Colleague.—Our mutual flattery.—Our first Disciples.—My own morals.—A "liberal Correspondent."—My mode of studying the Bible.—Interest in Sabbath schools.—Formation of a Sabbath school, and a Public Library.—Character of the Books procured.

ONE person, in particular, entered into all my views and sentiments, and sympathized with me at almost every step of my progress. He, too, had been led to "the light" in part, by study and effort in behalf of the young mind. Our meetings were not frequent, but always interesting; and perhaps the more so, *with our views*, from the fact that we made it our great business to encourage and flatter, rather than correct and improve each other. I have generally found that those persons are most benefited by social interviews who make it their business, at suitable times and places, to criticise each other's views, manners, opinions, writings, &c. This has not only been observed in others, but found true in my own case. But under the imaginary influence of "new light," "freedom from prejudice, illiberality," &c., my whole internal character and habits of feeling were strangely altered. Every thing but commendation and flattery was insipid; and doubts of my own infallibility were becoming not only unpleasant but almost intolerable.

At a certain time when my companion, *in Utopia*, called to see me, he brought a friend who had formerly been as thorough a disciple in what I called the "old school" as myself. He had, indeed, been farther than I, and sustained a standing—I believe irreproachably—in an evangelical church. I had gained access to him, both by conversation and letter, before this visit; and had already slightly shaken his faith. He was now assailed from a double battery. The unreasonableness of eternal punishment was the prominent topic, against which our efforts were directed, and our weapons seemed to make some impression. On parting, we congratulated him on his progress in the path of free inquiry, and ventured to predict that he would ere long taste the sweets of rational liberty and mental independence!

This prediction was, alas! but too well verified. My blood runs cold, when I think of the results.

This young man had received a pious education from an excellent mother and prudent father. The social influences to which he had been subjected were in the highest degree favorable, He had been united with an excellent church, and was apparently walking with them towards the house eternal in the heavens. His general reputation in the world, was that of an amiable, pious, promising young man. But possessing, in an eminent degree, the sanguine temperament, he was easily led to make an effort to start out of the common ranks of life by eccentricities of opinion, and in the same way readily seduced by the idea of "originality of character." It was at these vulnerable points that he was assailed, and in the end successfully. He is now in a distant part of the Union, at a point where any opinions, however heterodox, pass currently, provided there is no striking departure, externally, from the rules of morality.

Here, if his letters to his friends are an index to his sentiments, he is a rank atheist, of the school of Owen and Wright, living only for the present, neither expecting nor ardently desiring an existence beyond the grave which must finally cover him. I have written him occasionally, and without direct *preaching*—which I knew would be utterly vain—endeavored to touch his heart; but hitherto, so far as I know, without effect. I have little doubt that he will go through the "dark valley" with his present belief, and that in the day when the secrets of all hearts shall be made known to assembled worlds, it will be found that I have contributed in no small degree to the murder—no, not merely the murder, but the endless suffering of an immortal mind and heart. Great Parent of the Universe, what is man! And how fearfully tremendous are his responsibilities!

The inquiry sometimes arose in my mind, at this period, whether the influence of "improved," or "liberal" opinions had thus far been favorable on my own character. But the question was, almost of course, soon decided in my own favor. Indeed it appeared to me that my progress in knowledge and excellence had never been greater. Nor am I conscious, even now, that there had been, up to this period, any striking departure from correct moral habits,—I mean externally,—except in the points which have been already mentioned.

But there were two reasons why such a result was not to be expected. First, when a person is accused or suspected of holding heretical opinions, he has usually common sense enough to know that one principal means of repelling the charge is to *live down* the accusation. Secondly, it generally takes a long time, for even those opinions, whose tendency is the worst, to produce any very marked changes in the character of an individual who has been subjected, from childhood up to years of maturity, to the best of moral influences.

But although my morals had not yet suffered, there was a great change in my religious feelings. Prayer had become altogether formal, and was often neglected. The Bible was seldom opened, unless with a view to investigate some doubtful or disputed point. True, I attended an orthodox church, but it was more for the sake of passing current with the religious world than with a view to real improvement. There was, however, one more prominent reason for attendance. I had acquired the habit of criticising sermons pretty closely, and of finding much in most of them to support my own sentiments. Indeed, I was of opinion, at that time, that I usually derived much more benefit from a discourse which I did not believe, than from any other. And when I regard a sermon merely as an *intellectual* production, the result to this day, is often the same.

All this while I was an ardent friend of Sunday schools; more, however, for the sake of the intellectual and moral improvement which has hitherto followed in their train, than with reference to any higher results. But of my connection with these institutions, I shall have occasion to speak at large presently.

By a series of circumstances which it is unnecessary to mention, I had become acquainted by letter with a Unitarian gentleman at a distance, but without knowing at first what his peculiar views were on the subject of religion. He appeared to be a zealous friend of every measure which had for its object the improvement of our race, and as such I did not hesitate to hold correspondence with him. He, too, on the other hand, was pleased with many of my remarks; and forthwith concluded, as he afterwards stated, that I did not belong to the "old school." But he possessed knowledge enough of the human character as well as politeness enough not to obtrude his opinions, and it was sometime before he ventured to introduce the discussion of religious subjects at all. Gradually, however, they came up; and on many, if not most topics, our opinions were found to harmonize to so great an extent that I was surprised at the coincidence. Books and papers were kindly sent me on subjects relating to improvement, such, for example as temperance, infant and Sunday school instruction, &c.; and before long, tracts and discourses, which, though they did not embrace the distinctive tenets of "liberal Christianity," had a bearing on the subject. These I received and read with great pleasure.

While on this subject, I wish to observe that so far from supposing that the gentleman alluded to was engaged in a proselyting scheme all this time, I am of opinion, on the contrary, that this formed, at first, no part of his intention; but that his principal object was to oblige a friend and fellow-worker in the common cause of humanity, with whom he was so constituted by nature, and fitted by education, as deeply to sympathize. In fact, I have seldom met with a man—among those who make such loud pretensions on this subject—who seemed to me more free from a proselyting spirit.*

At length our religious opinions became mutually understood, and I obtained several tracts and other publications embracing the peculiar sentiments of Unitarians as set forth by the champions of that sect. "Liberal" as I was, however, and boastful of "free inquiry," so strong are the prejudices of education, that I think my feelings would even now have revolted at some of the views therein embraced, had I not been "pre-

---

* See Appendix, note A.

pared" for them. By the views which I had taken of human nature, of sin, and its punishment, I had rendered an *infinite* Savior unnecessary; and of course was not so much shocked to learn that no infinite atonement had been made! Every man who lived and suffered for his fellow-men, whether his life was cut short by it or not, I had long been accustomed to regard as *a Savior* to a greater or less number of his fellow-men, because he was a means of removing from the world a portion of its physical and moral evil. It was, on the whole, easy, therefore, to conclude that *the Savior of mankind, though he were a created and dependent being*, might be the means of ultimately saving so large a share of mankind from their sins, and consequently, from their punishment, as to justify the superiority which is assigned him in the holy scriptures.

I did not, at this time, read the Bible to ascertain what the *real facts* in the case were, but contented myself with the quotations made by the various writers whose works I perused. Nor do I remember exactly the steps by which I came to conclusions in favor of the sentiments of "liberal Christians;" nor how much time was taken up in the inquiry. This, however, I distinctly recollect, that from the moment I began to read, or repeat verbally, or by letter, the favorite texts of Unitarians, and especially to suggest my doubts to particular friends, from that very moment, my progress was rapid. There was in truth, no candid inquiry, "What does the *Bible* say," for I was familiar with most of the prominent texts used by controversalists, though I only recollected them in their insulated condition, without remembering their connection with other passages and other sentiments. In fact, the *seeds* of error had long since been sown in my mind, and any opinion, however novel, if specious in its appearance, was very likely to spring up under the "genial influence" of the *sunshine* of "free inquiry!"

The interest I took in Sunday schools, has already been briefly mentioned. They were regarded as an invaluable means—not so much of promoting or favoring personal piety, as of purifying and elevating the intellect, and of improving the tone of the public morals. It was in this view, that my labors were applied to this department of instruction for several successive seasons.

At this period—in the summer of the year 1827—libraries in Sabbath schools were becoming common; but the inhabitants of the village where I resided, seemed to regard them as the fanciful project of some innovator, and of very doubtful utility. With a zeal worthy of the cause, I plead loudly in their behalf, and at length persuaded them that a library was necessary.

On reviewing my career at this period, I am not a little surprised, that with such strong suspicions abroad of my heresy, I should have retained such a measure of the public confidence as I did, even of the *religious* public. But my exterior morality, ardent zeal, and ability to use the language of all sects, and make all believe that my creed was substantially the same as theirs, seemed to atone, in part, for my errors of opinion; and I was permitted to go on with my purposes.

A small Sunday school library was soon formed, partly by public contribution, and partly by donations of books; not without considerable sacrifice, however, both of time and money. But this sacrifice was made willingly, because along with it, I had often opportunity to introduce such books as I pleased; and notwithstanding the vigilance of others, not a few were rather "liberal" in their tendency. Most of them indeed were either of this description, or merely scientific; there were few of the character of Sunday school books generally, and some of them could scarcely have been deemed even *moral* in their tendency. The library, however, did good, as well as the

Sunday school: though both might have done much more good, had they been superintended by warm hearts, as well as zealous heads.

The *village* library, formed about this time, partook less of the character which I had endeavored to stamp on the library of the Sabbath school. My highest hope, with the generation already risen was, to keep religious books of every kind out of their hands; believing, and I still think justly, that no better way could be found to destroy the public confidence in evangelical views of religion, than to awaken their attention to the improvement of mere intellect.* At the time of which I am speaking, *my* intention was to prepare the way, in the best possible manner, for the introduction of "liberal" views. My object was not the public good *directly* (because I believed our religious systems incompatible with any considerable degree of improvement;)—but indirectly and remotely, through more *liberal sentiments.*

---

* Whether religious books—those which are strictly evangelical, I mean—should be admitted to our public or town libraries, I do not know. Perhaps there might be one library to which access might be had by every community, into which religious books should not enter. Still I think there should be libraries of some sort containing evangelical books, even if they cannot be sustained in any other way than by particular sects.

CHAPTER VI.

MY CORRESPONDENTS.

One of my letters.—Various efforts.—Advice of a "liberal" friend.—Conversation.—Education.

WITH orthodox correspondents on the subject of Sunday schools I was still regarded as quite evangelical. With "liberal" correspondents, however, I was justly regarded otherwise; as the following extract of a communication to one of them will clearly show. It was under date of September 12, 1827.

"I rejoice that there are, even in this land of thick darkness, a few to whom I can open my mind and unbosom myself—a few who think for themselves unshackled; a few who have not bowed the knee to the Baal of antiquity.

"Blessed be God, the Father of our Lord Jesus Christ, that a few of the inhabitants of ——— ——— belong to the army of the faithful; even to the one hundred and forty-four thousand that are redeemed from the earth. May your labors be successful, and may you win, by example and precept, till the whole neighborhood—yea, even the whole town,—receive the 'faith once delivered to the saints,' and practice accordingly.

"It is hoped that your exertions for the welfare of the world—especially the younger part of it, will be continued, and will succeed. For years I must confine myself to *correcting* errors, instead of preventing them. The monster prejudice is strong in this place, and I have little hopes of effecting any thing."

About this time, as nearly as I can recollect, it was proposed to have a "liberal preacher" come into that region, and present some of the least obnoxious of his sentiments. He was a warm friend of a certain benevolent scheme, and proposed, as his ostensible object, to lecture and distribute tracts on that subject, and whenever an opportunity offered, give a lecture on Unitarianism, or at least leave a few tracts on that subject. Though I was at this time nearly as "liberal" as he, yet I had made but few disciples, and those walked tremblingly along, afraid of the public sentiment, and perhaps conscious, too, that their weapons of defence consisted of a few cant phrases, or of borrowed language, which, like Saul's armor on David, might fail them in the hour of trial. On the whole I rejected the "disinterested" proposal of the gentleman, and told him that we were not yet prepared for him; that probably such a measure would defeat our dearest wishes and most anxious purposes. The contemplated missionary tour was at length relinquished.

It was not far from the same period that I sent for a few numbers of a weekly newspaper of the "liberal" kind, hoping I should be able, by their means, to introduce a little "light" among my benighted townsmen. But I did not like the paper, when it was received; it appeared dull and heavy. Besides it was too open in its views to suit my concealed mode of warfare. The numbers were accordingly returned to the editor, with the assurance that I *liked the paper*, but it was too "strong meat" for us in ——; though I hoped in a year or two, to furnish him with a considerable list of subscribers. His expectations, however, if any were raised, have not yet been realized.

Tracts, sometimes in considerable numbers, were sent me; and as I afterwards learned, my efforts were highly satisfactory to my distant "liberal" brethren;* and they already began to antici-

---

* To show the connection and the tendency of things, I may here mention that one of these gentlemen, then an editor, but since deceased, was exceedingly delighted with the efforts of

pate a golden harvest from the seed I was sowing. A brief article from my pen appeared in a periodical, which was highly praised by somebody, and I greedily swallowed the bait. It was in the form of a review of the "Memoir of Ann Eliza Starr," a small Sabbath school book. The thoughts were very well, but the style was miserable.

To guide me in my efforts, I wrote to my "liberal" friends for information. I begged them to tell me how fast, and under what circumstances, the "light" ought to be introduced. One of them in reply, observed that a man ought to labor to enlighten and improve society around him by degrees, only; assuring me that if I were endeavoring, as a surgeon, to restore the sight of a blind man, I would only admit the light gradually, and present objects in succession. The brightness of noon-day, he said, would blast the feeble powers of vision with excess of light—and the view of all things at once, might perhaps perplex forever. Just so, he thought it to be, with the mental and moral eye. We must impart truth as men could receive it.

Frances Wright, at Nashoba, and did not hesitate to call her, in his journal, an excellent woman. She by the way, paid off in the same coin. "I remark," said she, "with pleasure, the progress of liberal principles in New England!"

This advice had its intended effect. It made me more cautious of presenting sentiments which would be rejected with disgust; though it did not make me less solicitous to put people in the very paths which would lead to them. The general drift of my conversation was to show that there were no such tendencies to sin, in the infant, as would prevent his being trained up a Christian, if the necessary pains were taken. It was my belief that children were introduced into the world perfectly sinless, and as much inclined to good as to evil. Our great business, I said, was to "train them up in the way they should go," assured that just in proportion as this was effected, just in the same proportion would the prediction be realized, "they will not depart from it."

I did not openly deny that there was any other Divine agency in this, than in raising a stalk of grain or corn; but I made the denial in the company of intimate friends. The decrees of God, and several other points of theology, were rather ridiculed than reasoned against. To communicate the views which I have mentioned, I embraced every opportunity of conversation where I could find any person to hear me; and the number who would hear with apparent pleasure, was greater than I at first anticipated. The character of my audience, did not indeed always please me; for I found it oftener composed of the vicious and dissipated, than of the sober and virtuous.

As to circulating books and tracts, I was yet pretty cautious. A few were loaned secretly, but they did not seem to be very acceptable. Conversation interested people much more; especially if pains were taken to sneer at total depravity, original sin, eternal fire, a new heart, &c. The tract which I found most acceptable, and which seemed to produce the most effect on the minds of those who read it was, "The Three Questions Answered," "What is it to be a Christian?" "How am I to become a Christian?" and "How am I to know whether I am a Christian?" In this pamphlet the author—like Paley in one of his "sermons"—endeavors to show that there are some who do not need conversion, strictly speaking; such, he says, are already in "the kingdom," why then should they go out of it? All they have to do, in order to be members of Christ's kingdom, is to stay where they are. How this can be supposed to accord with the general language of Christ and his Apostles and followers,—that all are in danger of perishing, that Christ gave himself a "ransom for all," and that he made propitiation for the "sins of the whole world" is to me at present, inconceivable. But the writer of the tract is evidently *sincere*, and has made many converts to his error.

In conversation, it was a favorite practice with me to take the ground that those sects of christians with which we are not much acquainted, and against which we are apt to entertain prejudices, are much misrepresented. I affected to have examined the tenets of most or all of them, and to be able to set their doctrines in a proper light. In this way I embraced every possible opportunity of showing that the Unitarians, Universalists, Hicksites, &c., are strangely misrepresented. This gave me an opportunity of introducing my own favorite sentiments, and with much greater prospect of success than in any other manner.

It is true that this course of conduct subjected me to many inconveniences, as I was at first suspected of favoring the particular sect which I happened to be defending. But it was an evil which brought with it a remedy; for I was known, at length, to be in the habit of defending all, (all being occasionally misrepresented,) and as it was obvious that I could not favor the tenets of all *sects*, it was found rather difficult to fasten a charge. The preponderating sentiment, was, however, that I was more or less inclined to Unitarianism.

It has already appeared that I rested my hopes almost solely on the proper education of the young. It was in this view, and in reference to the peculiar character of the work, that in writing to one of my liberal friends about this time, after adverting to the various means which were employed for the promotion of liberal christianity, I gave it as my unhesitating opinion that *the only monthly journal then published on the subject of education, and which had just been established under the direction of Unitarians, was doing more for the cause of Unitarianism than all things else put together.** This remark, whether just or not, was, as I was afterwards told, extensively circulated; and while I was not a little flattered by the attention it received, I was not altogether pleased to have my letters carried about from place to place, or their contents made the subject of frequent remark. I liked the treason much better than the traitor.

At this period it was impossible for me to conceive how people could reconcile improved views

---

* My meaning was, that by its aid in improving mankind in early infancy, and keeping what I called "systems" and "creeds" out of the way, the work in question would indirectly promote Unitarianism. The journal referred to passed, soon afterward, into other hands.

of education, especially of *infant* education, with the old-fashioned theology. Had any one told me that within six years from that period, I should myself come to believe them perfectly compatible with evangelical sentiments, I could no more have believed his prediction, than had he said that Jupiter would become a comet in the same time.

So far as the existing fashionable systems of education tend to develope mere intellect, at the expense, or with the neglect of the body or the affections, the tendency will be anti-evangelical. And that such is the tendency of fashionable systems of education, I have already intimated ; and shall, in another place, attempt to prove.*

I am not ignorant that there are many who would bring up children without any religious opinions. They would implant good habits, by the force of example and other means, as early as possible, but leave them to form their creed for themselves, when they come to years of discretion. But is such a thing possible? By no means. What though you never say a word to a child in regard to your own, or any other religious opinions? Unless brought up like Caspar Hauser, he still has his creed. Not *written*, it is true ; but

---

* See Appendix, note B.

what is the difference? He just as surely imbibes opinions in *morals and religion* from his parents' character and conduct, as he does opinions in regard to his parents' mode of life, occupations, &c., &c. And those opinions, have as much influence on his conduct, as if they were written; perhaps even more. It is vain therefore, to talk of educating the young in a neutrality of opinion on moral subjects, more than on any other; and still more in vain to raise a hue and cry against creeds.

CHAPTER VII.

ANECDOTES.

Sickness of a young man.—Reflections.—Sickness and death of a disciple in error.—My own "management."

In the neighborhood where I resided, a young man was taken sick with a fever, which lasted nearly three months. As I was an intimate friend of the family, I often visited him. He was about twelve years of age. His relatives were eminently pious people; and both his father and grandfather, deacons in the church. The young man possessed a most excellent moral character, but had hitherto given no decided evidence of piety.

In the progress of the disease, some of the symptoms became alarming. The physician, who acquainted the parents with his state from day to day, at length candidly told them that the danger was much greater than it had hitherto been, though the case was by no means hopeless. *It was his general practice—and a judicious one too—to tell but one story*; he did not in the sick room represent the symptoms to be favorable, and then go into the next room and pronounce the patient very dangerous. The curious parents and friends, however, were not equally judicious in improving the warning given them, in relation to the young man ; and, in the present instance, particularly,— the results of his disclosures were deeply *unfortunate*. For no sooner was the word *danger* mentioned than they took the alarm at once, and what was worse, alarmed the young man.

A state of things was now produced which rendered the actual danger far greater than before. Sighs and sobs, and down-cast and dismal looks, —perhaps tears, also—and the cold wishes of parting friends, who visited him quite too often, told more plainly than words could have done it, that they looked daily and hourly for his dissolution. The prayers of pious friends at his bedside were frequent and ardent, and notwithstanding doubts in the minds of the parents of my own orthodoxy, I was once or twice called on to lead in these exercises. Nothing was more abhorrent to my feelings at this period than the idea of trying to benefit the souls of the sick in this manner ; but to gratify friends, and save my reputation, which, as an evangelical man, with them had been for sometime on the decline, I consented. There is no room for doubt that the disease was rendered much more formidable and protracted by these misguided, though well intended efforts of friends and relations—though the young man finally recovered, so strong is nature, in spite of us.

I was not slow to inform my "liberal" correspondents of this young man's case. The fact was that though he had been much exhorted in the hour of danger to look to the Savior for pardon, and often urged, in the moments of parental and neighborly anxiety to trust in him, yet he had uniformly, so far as I could learn, resisted their efforts, or at least answered their inquiries in a manner which only added to their distress.

The intelligence was interesting to my Unitarian friends on two accounts. First, they construed it into a triumph of liberal principles. Secondly, they were gratified to find my views of death-bed repentance so exactly corresponding with theirs.

It is not a little curious to observe with what eagerness our Unitarian brethren seize on every opportunity to announce to the world as an important discovery of theirs, that death-bed repentance is a rare occurrence—and still less frequently genuine. They seem to forget that among thousands of conversions which happened in Judea nearly eighteen hundred years before the time of Dr. Priestly, only a solitary instance of death-bed repentance is recorded. Even this was a man dying in full strength, instead of being worn out in body and mind with disease.

When some ignorant or misguided zealot advances a doctrine which not one in ten of his brethren believe, how often is it set down as a part of orthodoxy itself! This charge is not peculiar to Unitarians, it is true ; though I wish it were. But in a sect, who by their general language and the names and attitudes they assume appropriate to themselves nearly or quite all the "discrimination," and "candor," and "light," and "charity," and "liberality," and "*Christianity*," which the sun shines upon, such conduct is hardly generous. —Every where, for example, we hear much said about the terrible "decrees" of God ; when every one knows, or may know, that no consistent, intelligent, evangelical christians believe in any decrees which hinder a person from doing what he pleases.

My own prejudices were not a little strengthened by the circumstances connected with the case above mentioned. For believing, as I did, that *pure morality* and the *love of God*, or holiness, were one and the same thing, I could not help feeling pained at seeing an amiable, inoffensive, and as I *then* believed, *pious* young man, thus tortured to confess a belief which he neither understood nor could appreciate.

Let me not be understood as saying a word, even now, in justification of the course which was taken. My object has been to show that it has no more to do with *orthodoxy*, as a system, than with the moon. Fond parents—and too many who are not parents—among all sects which I have ever met with, are very apt to lay a great deal of stress on the *last words* and actions of their friends. Too many, like Balaam, would gladly " die the death of the righteous," who seem not very anxious to live a righteous life. It is not a doctrine peculiar to Unitarians that people generally " die as they live." It is a truth that forces itself upon every observing mind.

I say people *generally* die as they live. There are exceptions. A few disciples of error, and even a few christians seem shaken, at the approach of death ; but the majority, with as few exceptions as to all general rules, go out of the world quietly ; believing as they have done while they lived. If they have lived Catholics, they die so ; if Protestants, they go out of life such. If they have lived Universalists, Unitarians, Rationalists, Deists, or even Skeptics, they die so. If they have lived thoughtlessly, they also die thoughtless. Such, I say is the general fact, though this is no encouragement to continue in error or sin. Indeed it is, as it appears to me, a powerful reason why we should seek to know the truth, and practice accordingly, while we have life and health. Genuine death-bed repentance is possible, but never probable.

One man whom I began to number among my "liberal" friends, was near sixty years of age. He was moral, and professedly religious, but the particular church to which he belonged, was rather lax in its discipline; and a considerable part of its members manifested very little interest in experimental religion. They met, it is true, every Sabbath, and those who did not sleep, attended to the services. The intermission was chiefly spent in conversation on their ordinary occupations, and in noticing and censuring the faults of other individuals and churches. No man could find more fault with the doctrines of "depravity" and "election," as he called them, than my friend.

Within the last ten years of his life, a concurrence of peculiar circumstances had greatly contributed to increase his prejudices. He became quite censorious; though otherwise of a mild and amiable disposition.

In various ways he had received now and then a "tract." These he had perused with great interest. For sometime, however, he "endured," rather than believed. At length he partially "embraced." I am not aware that he ever openly rejected the doctrine of *Christ's divinity;* though even on this point, I am sure he was quite unsettled.

He was taken sick, and the physician, after several days of illness, pronounced his disease to be dangerous. He was not apparently much alarmed at first, but seemed willing to submit to it, as a kind of fatality.

As he was not only a neighbor, but a disciple of mine, I was often with him. The subject of religion, and of his own personal interest in it, occasionally came up, and he sometimes manifested much anxiety. I took unwearied pains, however, to quiet him, by assuring him that a man of his character could have no reasonable cause of alarm; or to divert him by introducing other topics of conversation.

I had three reasons for this. First, I was, for a time, strongly inclined to the opinion that he would ultimately recover. Secondly; it was a fixed principle with me, that in general the sick bed is not the place for conversation on religious subjects; and I still think they require rather the undivided energies of a person of health and vigor. But in the third place, I knew that in his debilitated condition there was some danger of his being doubtful in regard to his religious safety. This I thought would be fatal, in that region, to the spread of "improved" sentiments. A person's state of mind on his death bed may not, it is true, be a proper test of his character in the sight of God; but I knew that such was the belief of most people in that region, and I governed myself accordingly.

As the danger increased, and death drew near, he evidently became more and more anxious about his spiritual condition, and at the same time less able to attend to the subject with interest or profit. At length his physician pronounced him delirious—at least at certain seasons.

I was very glad to avail myself of this circumstance of delirium as an apology for any expressions which escaped him, which I found would make impression on the by-standers unfavorable to Unitarianism. Whenever he said he feared he was deceiving himself in his religious hopes, &c.; I was ready to represent him as more or less insane. I do not doubt, indeed, but he was so in some degree; though I think I was inclined to overrate the degree of mental aberration.

In spite of all my efforts, however, the neighbors would intrude. Every one—especially if he could do no good—was glad to come occasionally, and throw a cold and ghastly glance at him, (enough alone to frighten him) and in a pitiful tone of voice HOPE *he would be better to-morrow.* Now and then one would put the supposed all-important question—whether he felt prepared to die.

This constant influx of useless and worse than useless visitors to the sick bed of an individual, is exceedingly trying to a physician. And really, I could almost wish a rule were adopted in this country, which as I have some where read, prevails in Germany. A book is kept in the porch of the house, in some convenient place, in which the physician every morning writes down the state of his patient, very particularly; and when visitors call, they are referred to this book, where they enter their names. If any who call are desirous of rendering assistance, they write opposite their names what they wish to do, and when they will to do it.

But to return to my story. My friend was now evidently about to die. No minister had yet visited him, although for ministers to visit the sick, once during their sickness, is quite a common custom in that region. The pastor of the church to which he belonged, lived several miles distant. As

I found it would be useless to oppose the current, and on being consulted, I advised to send for him.

I was well acquainted with the character of the minister. I knew that he would place great confidence in my opinion; and probably follow my advice. As I could not be present when he came, and was fearful that the sick man, in his debilitated state of body and mind, would express such doubts or make such confessions as I did not wish, I sat down and wrote a line to the minister, begging the family to put it into his hands as soon as he arrived.

In this letter it was stated, briefly, that my friend's mind was in such a state that conversation with him would not probably afford much satisfaction to any one; and whatever others might think, it was my belief that it might diminish his chance of recovery;—begging him to be as brief in his services and hold as little conversation with him as possible.

The letter was delivered, and my project completely succeeded. The wife of the gentleman, however, appeared suspicious. Yet as she had never known or heard of any "concealment" or "duplicity" on my part, she was loth to believe even the testimony of her senses.

He had now become really and truly delirious, but the delirium was so great, and nature was so much exhausted, that little or no attention was paid to his expressions. Every now and then he repeated a kind of prayer that if he was in error he might be undeceived; but, whether he was rational or not, was unknown. He also manifested a strong desire to be reconciled to certain individuals with whom he had formerly had difficulties. In this, at least, he appeared to be quite rational. This state of things continued to the time of his dissolution.

Such were my feelings that I could not attend his funeral. Not that I supposed there had ever been any probability of his repentance after he was at first taken sick, but because the family were evidently dissatisfied, in some measure, with the course I had taken, and because I regreted that the cause of "truth" should require so much effort of concealment.

Not many months afterward, the bereaved companion of the deceased begged an interview with me on the foregoing subject. She candidly acknowledged that there were some things in my conduct which were to her a little unaccountable, and asked me to explain. With a brazen face and many smooth words, I partly succeeded in removing the difficulties which had arisen in her mind; but not entirely.

Finally, however, the mystery and doubt which, in the view of the neighborhood, hung over the affair, was in part forgotten; and it was not till a year or two afterward that a sense of duty compelled me to write a letter to the injured family, confess my faults, ask their forgiveness, and thus make the only restitution in my power. Subsequently to this, a personal interview gave me an opportunity of still further explanation.

I do not wish to be understood as intimating that I disapprove of all the principles by which I was influenced on the above occasion. But I must condemn, with unsparing severity, the concealment and duplicity to which I resorted.* It

---

* In the progress of my narrative I have more than once adverted to the causes of this effort at concealment, but without giving that attention to the subject which it merits.

When a man adopts unpopular opinions in religion,—unless it happens, as it may, that they are the truth, and unless the heart is strongly influenced by confidence in God,—as in that case it will be—there is a very great temptation to conceal; and not only to conceal, but to misrepresent. A person says, perhaps; "Why they say you don't believe in a Savior?" "Not believe in a Savior! to be sure I do," will be the reply; when the fact is that he reserves to himself the right of construing his language in his own way; and knows that

is improbable, however, that if repentance were necessary, there was vigor enough of body and mind, when the course of concealment first commenced, for the purpose. In similar circumstances, I should now advise, rather than endeavor to prevent religious conversation, in the early part of the disease. I mean I should do so with the permission of the physician.

But no ordinary circumstances should induce me to encourage a thing of this kind, unless the physician thought it best. When he is called, every thing which pertains to the social and moral, no less than the physical treatment of the individual, should be wholly left to him. He may be *requested* and even *urged*, but never opposed. If our confi-

---

according to the construction which the inquirer puts upon it, he does *not* believe in a Savior.

Thus a person is, not unaptly, led into the habit of stating his own views in langauge, which he knows will be construed quite differently from the manner in which he himself construes it;—and thus he is led, gradually, to misrepresentation and duplicity. A man, in this way, may belong to any and every sect he meets with; for he has only to quote scripture, in their own order and arrangement, and say that he believes it, without giving his own definition. This was the habit into which I was insensibly led, notwithstanding my early rectitude.

dence is misplaced, we should withdraw it at once. There are more physicians than one in the world.

There are undoubtedly periods, during the progress of chronic disease—and sometimes of diseases which are *acute*—in which the presence of a minister or any prudent christian friend would be salutary to the body as well as the soul. Great caution, however, ought to be used on this subject; and if it were wholly left to the good sense of the physician to prescribe, I am quite confident society would, in the end, reap a rich reward, and at the same time remove one prominent cause of that medical skepticism which, after all, it cannot be denied, does too frequently exist, and which may possibly be increasing.

CHAPTER VIII.

MY SENTIMENTS ON PRAYER.

External attention to religion.—Specimen of my opinions and mode of reasoning.—Their fallacy shown.

ALL this while, events were transpiring which could not do less than confirm the popular suspicions in regard to my orthodoxy. Still, however, I did not leave the place of my supposed concealment, but continued to shelter myself behind the language of compromise, evasion, and sometimes, I fear, of duplicity. My zeal in the cause of improvement—so far as the eye of external observation could judge—was even increasing. My occupation presented more difficulties than that of most men, and yet there were few, if any individuals in the community who paid greater attention to all the outward means of grace (the sacraments excepted) than I did. I was almost always at church seasonably, and at my post in the Sabbath school. Partly from conviction of its importance, I used for a year or two to kneel in the church during prayer, and stand during singing, although in these two respects, I was alone. In the family where I was a boarder, I obtained permission to attend family worship night and morning, and to attend to other religious duties. And although I was in part convinced of the importance of these duties, *as* duties, yet I was probably influenced in no small degree by a desire to repel, by my life and conduct, the growing public suspicions. The more these gained strength, the more persevering I was in the performance of these outward duties.

But while all this was going on in the external world, it may not be uninteresting to the reader to see what was within, and what title I had to the character which I claimed. The following paragraphs are extracted from a manuscript which was dated about the time to which the remarks I have just made, apply.

" Whether the practice *of depending on external objects* to excite the *spirit of devotion,* does not in the end, produce much more evil than good, is with me a question. I have sometimes thought that by using these artificial helps, we come into a habit of depending on them, and ultimately lose that portion of the real spirit of prayer which we previously possessed ; and that if prayer ever appears in language it should be a spontaneous thing, excited by the circumstances in which the supplicant is placed.

" We are, indeed, to pray without ceasing. This I understand to imply that we are constantly to live in the spirit of prayer ;—that in all our thoughts and feelings we are to wish and desire good to mankind, our enemies not excepted ; and in all our ways, words, and actions, endeavor to *promote* that general good. To do this, would be to pray without ceasing. Now whether *times* and *seasons* for prayer do not on the whole diminish our power as well as our disposition to pray without cessation, demands a doubt. That our feelings, and wishes should rise to such a pitch as to produce emotion, and even ejaculatory prayer, is perfectly natural ; and if emotions of any kind are desirable, they are desirable here. But there is a wide difference between that kind of prayer which is spontaneous, and that which is forced— compelled. And if compulsion has an unfavorable tendency, generally, how know we but its tendency is unhappy here ? How do we know but that while we force ourselves to attend prayer, statedly, as a duty, instead of having it excited by spontaneous feeling, we are fostering a spirit of hypocrisy, and bringing ourselves into a habit of taking up with the letter for the spirit—the shadow for the substance?

"I would not speak confidently on the subject. But it appears to me that so long as *formal* (that is, all but purely mental) prayer is considered of more importance than the spirit of prayer—that is, prayer without ceasing—so long will this never-ceasing prayer be declining in the earth. But while we neglect doing every thing in the spirit of prayer, our regard—our real heart-felt regard—for even *stated* prayer, whether public or private, must, it seems to me, be diminishing.

"Here I anticipate an objection, which at first view seems to carry great weight. Jesus, our exemplar, prayed; but did formal prayer diminish the spirit of prayer in him? I answer that I do not know. Perhaps he prayed formally much less than we are accustomed to suppose. There is, I believe, very little evidence that he prayed much in this manner. When it is said that he continued 'all night in prayer to God,' it means, doubtless, that he was more in the spirit of prayer all that night than at some other times. That he did pray formally, however, is manifest both from the facts as related by the evangelists, and from the practice of his immediate followers. And I do not know but it *did* diminish the spirit of prayer, even in Jesus. If facts seem to prove that such is the result of formal prayer at the present time, it is likely it was so then.

"Why then, it will be asked, did he practice it? I answer, 'because of the unbelief and hardness of heart' of his followers. He found them attached to a religion of forms. His object was to establish a religion of *spirit*. Now had he introduced his religion in all its purity at once, what would have been the consequence? He well knew; and he took a wiser course. He undertook to *reform their religion*. 'I came not,' says he, 'to destroy the law, but to fulfill it.' But, that his *ultimate* object was to establish a spiritual system,—a religion of the heart without forms,—is most certain. See Matthew v. 28. Here is one of the strongest proofs of the spirituality of his kingdom. Yet he conformed to the existing Sabbath—in some measure, at least,—and on some occasions prayed publicly. It was undoubtedly necessary, at that time, that he should do so; it *may* be necessary that the followers of truth should do so now. But it may, also, *be unnecessary*.

"Let me not be understood to assert that the Sabbath, or prayer, or religion, or human laws are to be neglected. It is because I estimate the *spirit* of these things highly, that I thus speak freely. It is because I would make every day holy, all things prayer, all things religion. The law of God I would have perfectly kept, but it is the *spirit* of the thing which is wanted; and I should not be surprised—if in my next state of existence I should be susceptible of surprise—to look down upon the future generations of our race, and find them obeying the whole law of God and man, *as written only in their physical, mental and moral nature.* But ere man can become so eminently spiritual—*immortal*—much must be done. Would that the friends of improvement—*the saviors of their race*—in the spirit of the great Savior, may be excited to constantly increasing diligence in the great and good work of promoting human happiness!"

I have introduced this long extract to show first, my inconsistency at that time; secondly, the progress I had made in the road to error.

For it will be recollected in the first place, that notwithstanding all I said and felt of the evil effects of formal prayer, I constantly practiced it both in public and in the domestic circle. It must be confessed, however, *I did not pray in secret.*

In the second place, it will be seen, very plainly, that I had by this time become quite a "liberal;" and indeed in a few points rather too liberal for some of my fellows. For not only had Christ become "Jesus," and "Jesus our example," and a Savior amongst many other *less* saviors—a great *Savior* merely—but he could, according to my views *compromise* ; or as my language might easily be construed, *conceal*.

Now is this all that might be gathered, in regard to my progress. I certainly did pervert scripture. This *does* represent Christ as praying *formally*, and that, too, often ; and I cannot think a person is justified in saying that when he continued in prayer all night to God, it only means "in the spirit of prayer." For if he merely prayed in secret, or rather in spirit, how could it have been *known* that he prayed at all, to those who contend (and it is a piece of the same system to make the claim,) that the writings of the evangelists are mere *records* of a revelation ? Indeed common sense, the best sense to bring to the interpretation of scripture, after all, would understand by the language of the evangelists that he prayed in word,—not every moment, to be sure—but at intervals, at the least, through the whole night.*

---

* Some commentators, I know, suppose the meaning of the scripture language to be that he continued all night in a **house** or **place** of prayer.

Once more. Not only are arguments here used, which, if they have any weight against formal prayer, are of equal weight against worship of any kind, and against the Sabbath and its ordinances,—but this ground is even taken. Every day, it is said, is to be made "holy; all things, prayer; all things, religion." But as there is undoubtedly a sense in which this is admissible by all, I went even farther. "Highly favored future generations" are to find "forms impede their progress." Of course they will be rejected. Why then, it might be inferred, shall not the "liberal" reject them now? Future generations are to obey the "laws of God" as "written in their physical, mental, and moral nature." Of course the Bible will be out of fashion.—Why shall not those of us who have cantoned out to ourselves Goshens of "light and liberality" regard it, even now, as an old fashioned book? They are, then, to be *immortal!* Yes, reader, immortal below the sun! what use, then, in looking above the sun for immortality? "Let us eat and drink," not like beasts it is true; for this would be disreputable—but let it be our main object to enjoy all we can, physically, mentally and morally—"for to-morrow we die."

These are, it seems to me, natural inferences from the foregoing premises—were the premises, themselves, admissible. Not the inferences of the mass of mankind, to be sure; for theirs would be still more sottish and beastly; but those of the more elevated and intelligent.

Reader, are you nearly disgusted? Well, I do not wonder, for I am. I would not weary your patience, but this account seems to me, one of those *prophylactics*, as physicians call them, which the present corruption of the moral atmosphere requires; and I cannot but hope it will be useful in saving you from that dreadful disease which had well nigh destroyed my own soul. May my example serve as an awful beacon to warn you to avoid the rocks on I split!

To the young especially, I hope my narrative will be salutary. Next to the treachery of your own deceitful hearts is that treachery which deludes you into a spurious "free inquiry," a spurious "liberality," "rationality," &c. I have seen an end of all this; and in the language of the wise man can assure you that it is nothing but "vanity and vexation of spirit." I must be permitted to say once more, however, lest I should be misunderstood, that I am not the enemy but the friend of free inquiry, reason and liberality; though not of every thing which claims these good names. I am fully convinced that there is nowhere less of either of these than among those who make the loudest and most exclusive pretensions to them. But not to inquire freely, reason carefully, and be liberal and charitable, in the true sense of these terms, is treason, almost, against Him who gave you your faculties. Let me especially urge you to use your common sense. For this, too, you are accountable. Let it go with you in your inquiries on the subject of religion, as well as accompany you elsewhere—and do not suffer yourselves, by neglecting and despising so precious a boon, to sink in the blackness of darkness forever.*

To resume my subject. There seems to be a war against formal prayer, Sabbath keeping, &c., in the foregoing paragraphs; but why? Do not words and the posture of the body influence the mind? For my own part, I have no doubt that in any given instance, he will possess most of the spirit of prayer, other things being equal, who makes the most of language, posture, &c.—provided his course of conduct does not become theatrical. But suppose the supplicating posture, and the language of confession, thanksgiving, entreaty, &c., were universally excluded, how long

---

* See Appendix, note C.

would the spirit of these things remain? Those persons who oppose all prayer but what they call praying in spirit, seem to forget a doctrine which is usually quite a favorite with them, viz. that "example is better than precept." They even hold that religion is principally to be inculcated by example. But if prayer must always be purely mental, or rather must consist in a general feeling of benevolence; and if example is the only or principal mode of teaching others to pray, all prayer, whatever, would cease with the next generation. The same remarks are true—and strikingly so,—of the keeping of the Sabbath, of attention to Baptism, the Lord's Supper, &c.

We are moreover directed to "let our light shine." But how can it shine, if it is never to be embodied into words or actions? Our love to God, for example—how could our light shine, in this respect, if there was no *evidence* to the world around us, in our language or actions, that we ever thought of him?

CHAPTER IX.

PROGRESS IN ERROR.

My Rationalism.—Interview and discussion with a Minister.

When an individual has once set out in a course of error, there is no telling where he may end. All vices and error, as well as virtues, are relatives. Having embraced one error, you are more likely, other things being equal, to admit another, and sometimes a whole company of them at once. This tendency in our nature is highly useful when properly directed; otherwise its results are equally injurious.

Having lowered the scriptures and the Savior to suit my own convenience, it was now perfectly natural to take another step. I had robbed him of his *darling* attribute, mercy, by reducing the Son to the character of a mere creature; and now I proceeded to strip him, one by one, of his other attributes. The following is a short article which I wrote on the Divine *immutability*.

"Throughout the material world, all things are mutable. Even the mind of man, partaking as it does of a higher nature than that of other animals, is subject to change. We are not the same yesterday, to-day, and forever. When we review our past lives, how are we struck at the difference between our present views and feelings, and those of some former period! We can scarcely believe we are the same beings. We think ourselves right now, though formerly wrong. But why? If our sentiments have altered during the last ten years, who shall guarantee their immutability for ten years to come? Why are we so fond of considering ourselves as 'being already perfect?' Simply, I think, because we have been taught, time immemorial, to worship an immutable Deity.

"The character of man has always borne some proportion to the character of the Deity he has contemplated. Or to place the subject in a clearer point of view, man, individually and collectively, rises higher in the scale of excellence, the higher the standard at which he aims. And to the greatest possible excellence—the greatest at least of which we can conceive—we give the name of Deity. Now immutability is said to be one of God's attributes. Hence is it not highly probable that a belief in this doctrine, and associating it with other attributes of the Deity, has led *men* to aim at immutability, and to deem it derogatory to their character to be found mutable?

" But does not our very happiness depend in a certain sense, on our capacity to change? What is it that makes man nobler than the beasts that perish? Is it not the principle of improvement—the power of changing his condition? And shall we dread change?

" For my own part, I rejoice that I am mutable. I might have been formed an unchangeable being;—I might have been formed susceptible of change, but incapable of changing myself. But I find myself both susceptible of change, and able to change myself. Blessed prerogative! May it never be abused. And should I find that the worship of a God who changes not, tends to impede my progress in the career of improvement, I will conclude that the character of the Deity is, in this respect, misunderstood. That view of God or religion which tends most to raise man from the depravity into which he has fallen, must be the truest. ' By their fruits ye shall know them,' is a rule of universal application."

It is obvious that *this* extract, like those which I have before made, contains many just remarks;

but it is also obvious, that it closes with what in Germany would perhaps pass very well for Rationalism ; but which in this country deserves a more opprobrious epithet. The Germans, many of them, will not believe in the eternity of future punishment, because it appears to them inconsistent with God's general character. But are we not in duty bound to take the character of God as he has revealed it ? " Thou thoughtest verily, that I was such an one as thyself ; " but will it be an extenuation of the crime, that we *thought* so ? How absurd to measure God by ourselves ;—to erect a tribunal of our own by which to try the Governor of the universe ! But to resume my narrative.

Meeting with an old friend one day—a minister—he said he had heard of my *socinianism*, and begged me to tell him if the common reports were well founded. I assured him that they *were not* ; that I did not—I thanked God—belong to any *sect*, unless it were to the " general assembly of the saints :" that I thought the time had come when every friend of God and man ought to stand aloof from sect—or rather ought to form a sect by himself.*

---

* See Appendix.

We entered at length, into a pretty free discussion of principles; in which however, the arguments were rather superficial on both sides. But my friend had the advantage; for in setting out, I had made a concession which I did not intend to make; viz., that there had been a tremendous "fall of man" somewhere; and this being admitted, it requires no great art to drive a person holding the principles I then held, to close quarters. One liberal friend who understood this matter better than myself afterwards cautioned me against making this concession; for if I did, he said, I could not defend my position.

My antagonist at length pressed me so hard that he drove me off from Unitarian ground entirely. I, however, plainly told him I did not care whether I thought of a future world, or any beings or objects beyond this life, for five years to come. "Our great business," I said, "is to be like God. Now God is supremely selfish, *does all things for his own glory*—in order therefore, to be like him, I must do all things for *my* own glory. But the way, to promote *my* glory, is to promote the good of mankind in the greatest possible degree. Just in proportion as I can increase the general good, my own individual happiness will be increased; for my own happiness must always rise or fall with that of the general mass of mankind. Again; to increase the happiness of mankind in the greatest possible degree, I must concentrate all the powers of my mind and the affections of my soul on *them*—not on higher beings. If I think of superior beings and superior worlds, my attention is, for the time being, diverted from the main point. It is impossible to make progress with our eyes on earth, heaven and hell, at once. Would we avoid hell and attain to heaven, let our whole souls be fixed on this world. Let us make this a heaven—let us make a sort of immortality here below. In no other way can we carry ourselves and our fellow beings so rapidly towards an immortality of bliss above, as in this."

These extravagances, were a little startling. Both my friend and another gentleman who was present expressed their detestation of such sentiments. I strenuously defended them, and with not a little success; for it was a view of the subject which was rather new to them. Finally, however, I was startled myself. I left them, and meditated how I should retrace my steps, for I found I had gone too far. I was not aware at this time, that some Unitarians and many Universalists, I mean such as are nominally so, were of the same opinion. I thought I had discovered a "great truth," such as Dr. Channing so often discovers and announces to the public.

You will do me the justice, however to remember that I did not consider this as "forgetting" God. By no means. I considered myself as yielding prompt obedience to his commands. These commands as indicated in the volume of nature, and in so much of Revelation as "agrees" with it, seemed to me to say; "Consider how you can best accomplish my purposes, and promote my glory. When your mind is made up, go forward. Do not so much as think of me till you have carried your plan through; for it will only distract your attention, and retard your progress."

How far removed this is from the spirit of humble intelligent piety which the devoted and zealous christian fixes upon as his standard alike of duty and enjoyment, I hardly need to say. What sort of relation, for example, could subsist between teachers and pupils, or parents and children, where the children were expected to drive every thought of the parent or teacher from their minds for years, months, or even days? Would not this be to make a mockery of parental affection? To *have* parents and teachers, and to obey, love, and honor them, and yet only think of them once a year, or once in five years! It is an absurdity. And is it not at the least as great an absurdity, to forget the Parent of all for a series of years? You might as well blot out not only the word *affection*, but *the thing itself*, from under the whole heaven.

Every day is a miniature life. It has its infancy, its youth, its maturity, its age,—may I not say, its death? Then follows a resurrection, and another day or miniature life succeeds. Nothing appears to me more obvious than that every day must embrace, to a very great extent certainly, all the duties of life. Every affection which a human being ought to cherish at all, should be cherished every day. And I do not hesitate to say that no one, whether ten years old or fifty, can pass a whole day, without thinking of his parents, and yet not diminish his love for them. No more do I believe that any individual can safely spend a whole day without thinking of God. Every morning at the least, he is bound to lay his plans with reference to his will. And how many times in the progress of the day, nay, how constantly should the love of God call forth our gratitude, awake our reverence, confine our confidence, and fix our devotion!

Has God said, Son give me thy heart only

once in five years? Has he said; Promote my glory by forgetting me, except occasionally, or at long intervals; and only think how you can best serve yourself? Or has he taught us both by the precept and example of his Son to do every thing according to his will; and to remember him in all things and under all circumstances?

Why then did I fail to make this conclusion at the time above mentioned? Because I had adopted the principle, as a leading one, that the scriptures could teach us nothing in advance of our experience. For example; when experience has taught us that " Blessed *are* the peace makers;" then we know, I used to say, that the passage in Matthew which affirms *this*, is truly " revealed." But until our experience has taught us a doctrine, no such doctrine can properly be said to be revealed to us. A given chapter in the Bible may record twelve or twenty doctrines, but they are of no service as a revelation to us, till we have tested the truth of them by experience.

Strange indeed it was, as it now seems to me, even on the principles I then adopted, that I did not perceive how there may easily be such a thing as the true believer's realizing or experiencing, in a peculiar manner, the presence of God, in proportion to the intimacy of his communion with

MY RATIONALISM. 111

him; or in other words according to the growth and elevation of his piety. But so it was; I did not perceive it.

Thus, while I professed to believe in a revelation, I believed it in such a manner as to make it no more a revelation than any other book, unless it contained *more truths* than any other book; and nothing is more obvious than that this is equivalent to believing in no revelation at all. Yet I am well assured that I was not alone. A number of highly intelligent "liberal" Christians at that time held to the same, or nearly the same principle. That they all did, or even a majority of them, I do not believe; for I have more respect for their understandings than to believe it. And that *any* one *now* does, although only four or five years have passed, is quite another question, for their creeds are no more fixed than Dr. Priestly's was; and they often vary them as much in five years as he did his.*

Hence as has been said before, I was both a

---

* Dr. Priestly said he was at first a Calvinist, but afterwards became *liberal*. Proceeding onward, he at length, came to the conclusion that Christ was as fallible as Moses or any of the prophets. He candidly says; "I do not know when my creed will be fixed."

believer in revelation, and an unbeliever—and the same was true of every thing else. There was scarcely a doctrine drawn from the Bible, by any sect, but I could say I believed it, meaning in my own way.—In other company, I could also say, most conscientiously, that I disbelieved it—reserving to myself the right of explanation. I have since wondered, a thousand times, how I could so impose upon people; and still oftener, how I could reconcile such a course, to my sense of honesty or propriety. Gradually, however, this habit of saying a thing with a view to have it understood in a certain manner and reserving to myself the right of interpreting it in a different manner, so grew upon me that it was extended into other matters, and I found my regard for truth in the common concerns of life diminishing. It was now for the first time *suspected* that my "liberal" sentiments had an unfavorable influence on my moral and religious character, though even now I did not fully admit it, because I was *unwilling* to do so.

It was not long, however, before other circumstances confirmed my suspicions. My supposed converts made no progress. They would hear my remarks; (for I spent a good deal of breath among them) read my books, or rather those which were furnished me "to make a wise use of;" and bestow large censures upon other doctrines and sects. But as to doing anything for the promotion of "liberal principles," they would not lift a finger. This tried me—but I was not discouraged. I still, on the whole, believed—or rather tried to believe—the fault to be in myself, or the manner in which I proceeded, rather than in the doctrines which I taught.

CHAPTER X.

MY VIEWS OF REVIVALS, &c

More facts in regard to my early life.—On conscience.—A disputatious turn.—My studies.—Character of my books and associates.—Encouraged by the "liberals."

THE following extract from a letter written about this time, will show, in some measure, how I regarded revivals of religion.

"A conference of the churches was held here a short time since, and was immediately followed by a revival; but the work seems not to make very great progress. Perhaps by example, if precept has had no agency, I have been the means of saving a few souls from the rack; at the same time that *I* suppose they have been making progress towards heaven and happiness."

In regard to saving people "from the rack," I must do myself the justice to observe that I had reference, more particularly, to a class of people who are "almost persuaded" to become Christians, but, as they cannot assign any day or hour when they began to take a deep interest in religion, they remain in suspense between the world and God. My belief was that such ought to join the church at once; and that the revival doctrines were apt to discourage them from doing so, and keep them still longer in suspense. And although I cannot to this very hour, avoid sympathizing deeply with this class of the community, yet I can by no means justify the opposition of *heart*, which I felt *to the revival itself.*

Before I go farther with my narrative, I must be allowed to advert to certain facts and events of my early life, which I have hitherto purposely omitted; but which it now appears to me, ought to be made known to the reader.

I had early discovered in myself a propensity to take things upon trust, and had as early endeavored to counteract it. In doing this, however, I had gone almost to the extreme of taking *nothing* upon trust; and it was frequently in my own estimation, a sufficient cause for rejecting or opposing a thing, that it was generally received. Partly in this view I disliked the sports, the levity, nay, even the innocent and healthful gayety of my own playmates; and though I sometimes joined them, my conscience almost always reproved me on account of it.

I am at a loss to determine what will be said to this by those who think we cannot err so long as we act up to the dictates of conscience; a doctrine with some people highly popular. Now although we can hardly be justified in acting *contrary* to her dictates, yet nothing is better proved than that conscience, for want of being properly trained or enlightened, may approve of things which are contrary to the laws of God and man; and that so far as this result is the consequence of our *own* neglect, we may be and often are guilty before God in doing things which conscience fully approbates.

What contributed greatly to the formation of a habit of opposing every thing which happened to be popular, was the discovery that the rest of mankind, as well as myself, were for the most part led by tradition, custom, and the current of public sentiment; and that even on the commonest subject few could give any substantial reasons for their opinions or conduct.

Thus the foundation was laid for a habit of criticising upon every object, opinion, or act which came within my sphere of observation. Gradually I became thoughtful—and not only thoughtful, but pensive, and sometimes melancholy. I had already begun to allow my mind to expatiate on an improved state of things; and to dwell on Utopian projects, and Utopian regions.

If a thing was generally approved, I disapproved; if my companions were going to join a party, I had objections to it; if an individual was commended, I found something to mention as a drawback upon his general character; if a person was censured, I could find in him good traits of character, or at least could believe that they *might* be found; if a book was praised, I usually found means to condemn it; if my fellow youth were cheerful and gay, (as youth commonly are) I was for this very reason grave. Indeed I became, at length, grave constantly and habitually; and though my habit of opposing every thing did not generally please, my gravity was regarded by the *old* and the *middle aged* as a mark of wisdom; an error into which these two classes of the community are perpetually falling, greatly to the injury of all.

Whether in connection with all this, there was not much personal vanity, and an habitual desire of attracting attention by standing out of the ranks of the mass of mankind, perhaps the reader can determine better than myself.

As I advanced towards manhood, the habit of defending those whose character and opinions appeared to me to be misrepresented, grew into the habit of taking the side of sects and parties, whose principles or practice appeared to me to be misunderstood; and I made it a rule, as I have already intimated, always to defend any party, sect, or individual thus situated, whenever there was a greater probability that in so doing I should do good, than that I should injure myself.

Sometimes when I had gone as far as justice required, my success, and perhaps *a little vanity*, led me to go farther, for the sake of argument or for the pleasure of victory. " Perhaps," I would say " the Methodists (or whatever sect it might be) might meet your argument thus;" going on to defend their sentiments for them as well as I could.

This is a dangerous practice; and I cannot avoid repeating the warning I have before given especially to youth, not to venture a step on such ground. Let parents, too, discourage their children from disputation for the mere pleasure of exhibiting their talents. Few practices, I say confidently, are more dangerous.

The more a sect was spoken against, the more anxious was I to know what defence they would make. Now it was that I procured such books as Hannah Adams's View of all Religions. The

Universalists, in particular, attracted my attention. It was about this time, too, or a little earlier, that I met with the Unitarian Magazine, mentioned in a foregoing chapter.

My fondness for examining both sides of a question, though it had an excellent bearing on my character in many respects, insensibly led me into a *controversial*, rather than an *inquiring* spirit. But while controversy, carried to a certain extent, is highly useful, the spirit of controversy gradually deadens all moral sensibility. Controversies conducted for the *sake* of controversy, or carried to excess, seldom fail to injure the parties concerned, although the surrounding world may derive great benefit from them; but if all were to become thoroughly imbued with the spirit of disputation, religion and even morality would soon expire. Yes, were such an event possible, I am fully convinced that the " gates of hell " would thus ultimately prevail against even christianity!

During the subsequent years of my life, I mean after I began to aspire to the character of a Free Inquirer, I read all the Universalist periodicals and other " liberal " works I could procure; and some of the writings of the Swedenborgians and Roman Catholics. Few of these last, however, presented themselves. In regard to the works of the Unitarians, I thought myself fortunate. All or nearly all of the writings of Channing came under my notice, and not a few of those of Dewey, Follen, and the ministers of Boston. I also gained access to some of the works of Priestly.

With the views of Owen, both father and son, Wright, Jennings, Kneeland, Brownson,* &c., in this country, and Taylor and Carlisle, in England, I was also acquainted. With such works as Godwin's Political Justice, Voltaire, Mirabeau, Wolstoncraft, Roland, Rosseau, Paine, Cooper, and Jefferson, I was partially acquainted. Pope's Essay on man, which I considered, and still consider as belonging to the same class, was also studied; and subsequently the novels of Bulwer, which, however intended, appeared to have a tendency not unlike the foregoing.

With the *enlightened deists*, as they were sometimes called, of New Harmony, New York, and Philadelphia, and subsequently with those of Boston, perhaps few men in the country kept up a better acquaintance. I was not only familar with their periodicals, but with the books which

---

* This gentleman has since become, as he calls himself, a believer; but it is difficult, I suspect, for any one but himself, to say *what* he believes.

they commended, some of which are so bad that I should now be sorry to mention them.* In reading them, however, I never intended to adopt their sentiments any farther than they appeared to me just; but I read them for the sake of the truth I supposed they might contain. "Who would value a jewel the less," I used to say, "because he found it on a dunghill?" But I was so much startled, and withal interested in some of their bold statements, that I used occasionally to mention them. This called forth severe remarks, some of which were just, and others unjust. In defending them from the latter I was inclined, as usual, to go too far; and thus I gradually began to imbibe their sentiments.

But while my *head* was getting among the *enlightened deists* or *free-thinkers*, my *heart* was with the *Unitarians*. With the Universalists and Swedenborgians and *Christians*, I had less sympathy; they appeared to me ignorant, and their views low, obscure, or mystical.

It should also be mentioned in this place that I

---

* One of them, for example, I will mention. It was entitled "*Ecce Homo*," or Behold the man! treated the Savior in a manner which to me seems blasphemous. Skeptics generally speak well of the moral character of the Savior; but not so by any means with the author of *Ecce Homo*.

read several volumes of the works of Dr. Rush, among which were his treatise "On the Mind," and his "Account of the yellow fever" in Philadelphia. I have always been much pleased with the moral and religious views of Dr. Rush, generally, but there are a few of his remarks which a *visionary* might *wrest* to serve the purposes of human "perfectability." Some of the French physiological works fell into my hands, and from these too I collected materials for my "castle." All the new works on education seemed to me most decidedly in favor of the "*free inquirers*," especially the works of Pestalozzi; and every thing on physical education. It was at that time as great a mystery to me how a person could be *orthodox*, and yet be friendly to improvement in education, as it now is how any one can entertain improved views on this subject, without embracing orthodox sentiments.

When I heard of an individual, under forty years of age, who entered into the *spirit of the times*, as I called it, and especially into the subject of education, I counted as surely on his following the course I had taken, as if I had seen him on the way. This sometimes involved me in difficulty; for it led me to presume (in corresponding with him) on concessions which he often rejected with indignation.

Of all the Universalists and Unitarians I still felt pretty sure. My only fear was that we should push forward the work of " emancipation " prematurely. Taking the world as it was, I thought, that even the Unitarians, or at least some of their champions, were letting out the light rather too fast. Regarding them as a body, however, I thought them pretty safe, considering them the half-way house to truth. To those who were disposed to follow any sect, here, it appeared to me, was a good resting place for a while; but those who were willing to live *above* sect I thought ought not to wear the claims even of "liberalism." In writing to a correspondent whose views did not widely differ from my own, I said :—

"I cannot but think the Orthodox are letting in the light about fast enough. I am fearful that the liberal are going faster than human nature will yet bear. However, I hope we shall see all things work together for good. Do wear that yoke which is easy, and carry that burden which is light, rather than the galling yoke of party or sect, even the *Unitarian.* I know the Unitarians say many good things, but I am afraid mankind cannot bear them now. It seems to me that milk rather than meat, is needed at present."

In full confidence that the Unitarians would

eventually pursue what I regarded as the right road, I could not help sympathizing with an aged and *enlightened* deist in New York, who on reading the sermon delivered by Dr. Channing at the ordination or installation of Mr. Ware, immediately raised his spectacles, and in a tone of confidence extolled it to the skies, observing ; " *In five years, the Doctor will be with me.*"

Some of my friends furnished me with a long list of the names of gentlemen in New England, whose views were favorable to improvement, and whom they and I already began to number among the liberal, the enlightened, the intelligent, and the inquiring. I knew also the range of free inquiry, and rejoiced in seeing *so many noble-minded men* starting up, all over the country, and asserting their mental independence ; for if I could not go the whole length with them, I believed that when further inquiry had corrected their opinions, they would go with me :—and I already looked forward to the organization of a society whose influence and efforts should reform the world, and bring it back to Truth and Nature.

What that society ought to be in its external form, I had not as yet thought. There are several systems, now agitated, or plans commenced, which would have partially satisfied me, but not entirely. All these, or nearly all, began with the half spoiled adult, and I wished to begin with infants and children. Ballou and Fourier would have come nearer my wishes, perhaps, than the Shakers, or Owen, or St. Simon. Nevertheless, I could not have entered upon the plan of Fourier with all my heart, had it, at that period, been presented to me.

CHAPTER XI.

CHURCH CONFERENCES.

Opposition to these.—One family with which I was intimate.—Specimens of my manner of talking to them.—The family well nigh ruined.

About this time church conferences began to be introduced; and on one occasion, a considerable number of delegates from neighboring churches assembled in the town where I resided. Revivals of religion had often followed these meetings in that part of the country, and great effort was made by the Congregationalists of my neighborhood to produce similar results.

In opposing these efforts, I had a few associates among those whom I began to reckon as converts to "liberal" principles, besides which a considerable number of Episcopalians stood ready to second my exertions. These were, for the most part, very good people; but James was their especial favorite, because he insisted on good works. They seemed to forget that he was a thorough-going revivalist; that he spoke highly of human exertion to convert *one* "sinner from the error of his way;" and therefore could not be supposed to think human efforts to convert *scores* or *hundreds* of *less* importance.

No matter about *consistency*, however, when a point was to be gained. We believed it best to oppose the revival. Not for fear it would make men better, but because we thought it would make two or three worse, while it made one better.*

Some of us took " Good works" for our text. Others, " Six days shalt thou labor." Some of us undertook to retail thread-bare stories of the evils of revivals, which might or might not have been true.

In a day or two after the conference closed, it was reported that a considerable number of persons in various parts of the town were awakened to a sense of the importance of salvation. In short, there was quite a revival for so small a place; and although it was in some respects injudiciously conducted, it was apparently productive of good.

But the opposition made by myself and others, roused the opponents of evangelical truth. And what mortified me not a little, was, that of those

---

* We were sincere in all this. We really doubted the final utility of revivals. Sincerity, however, is no test of soundness of sentiment.

whom I had reckoned as favorable to "liberal" principles, the greater part manifested by their bitterness against the doctrines usually called evangelical, and against revival measures, that I had only strengthened their prejudices, without material benefit to themselves. They did not appear to "love their neighbor," any better than before.

As to the effects of my principles on my own mind and heart, I had, up to this time, thought them favorable. A friend asked me, one day, if I had carefully watched the state of my own mind and heart, to ascertain the effect which liberal views produced. I told him I had, and that I had great reason to rejoice at the result. It will be seen, however, in the sequel, that I was deceiving myself.

There was one family to which I had access and the opportunity of unbosoming my feelings, without the fear of being betrayed. None of them were religious people, unless it were the lady. She was an Episcopalian, and a person of decided piety; and by no means bigoted.

In this circle I used to spend hours and days— perhaps I might say *weeks*, in the whole, in endeavoring to inculcate "improved views." The father of the family was rather hostile to religious truth. One purpose at which I aimed, was to bring him over to a "better system" than that which had excited his prejudices; and I verily thought, for some time, I should succeed. But the old gentleman was too cunning for me. The more I conceded to him, the more he claimed; and while I yielded many points for the sake of getting him to yield a few of his, I found him only more strongly fortified in his errors, and less disposed to relinquish his objections to Christianity, than before.

When he urged his inability to change his heart, and said that according to the views commonly taught, it was of no use for him to attempt to do any thing himself, and that he must wait till he was *wrought upon*, I used to say: "When you feel an inclination to reform your life, then the Holy Spirit is operating upon you, and it is then you ought to go forward."

If he asked what he ought to do, my reply was; "Do what you know to be right. Cease to do evil,—Learn to do well,—Observe the dictates of your own conscience, and learn to obey them." But all the directions I gave, had reference to only the second table of the law; "Thou shalt love thy neighbor, &c." As to the love of God, I said little or nothing about it; or if I did, it was a merely speculative love to which I referred—as cold as a New England winter.

The following is a specimen of the course of remark I used to adopt. It developes views still less satisfactory to an inquirer after truth, than those just mentioned; and exhibits evidence of a rapid approach towards skepticism.

"We hear much said about God. Now God means *good*, and good is *God*. Devil means *evil*, and all evil is *devil*. Just in proportion as you can get rid of evil, by forming good habits, just in the same proportion, you are delivered from the bondage of the devil; and 'God dwells in you, and you in God.' Again: hell is bad feeling; heaven is good feeling, or mental and moral pleasure. Your great business is to get rid of the devil, and make your way to God as fast as possible. At present, you have much of Satan and the place of the damned within you. Be it your great business to expel all this, and supply the place with God and heaven.

"In order to do this, it is by no means necessary that you should *reflect* much on the subject, you have only to form your plans, and reduce them to settled habits. Nor is it necessary to *think* much about gaining heaven or escaping hell. You are in heaven or hell now; no matter whether you think of *any other*, these five years. Nay, more, you will probably make more progress—

will secure more heaven, and escape more hell here—and consequently more hereafter, by avoiding the thoughts of any world beyond this. Make this world heaven; create an immortality here, instead of looking for one beyond the sky.

"This, it will be said, is *infidelity*. By no means. I believe that when we have done all this; have secured God and heaven and immortality here, we shall go on, as a matter of course, to secure more and more of them beyond the grave. I believe that he who gets the most of heaven here below, will have the most of it in the future world; because he will be the farthest advanced towards perfection when he enters it. The infidel, on the contrary, would make this world heaven, and look for his immortality here, because he expects nothing *beyond* this world. We go together, then, as you see, a little way; but we separate afterwards, as widely as the poles.

"As to seeking Divine aid, the truth is about thus. When you have any good or proper feeling, that is Holy Spirit, or Holy Ghost. The more you are actuated by proper feelings and dispositions, the more you will improve in this respect, or in other words, the more you will be influenced by the Holy Spirit."

In a strain not unlike this, interspersed with

severe censures on those who hold different opinions, I have sometimes talked with the utmost earnestness an hour or two, and verily thought I was sowing good seed; such as would spring up, and bring forth a hundred fold. Alas! how have I been disappointed!

The person to whom I have just referred, has not only been made no better as a parent, husband, neighbor, or citizen, but rather worse. Nor have his prejudices against the Bible, or religion, or its ministers, been removed in any degree, but increased and strengthened. Nor did I benefit his family; on the contrary, I positively injured them, from the eldest to the youngest—the mother alone excepted. On her I could never perceive that I made much impresssion.

There was one other effort. I procured the lectures which Frances Wright delivered in some of the principal cities of the United States, and read some portions of them to my friend's family. They interested me so much, that I sometimes read with tears in my eyes; at others, I read and wept alternately. All to no purpose, however; my hearers did not sympathize with her. They only felt more prejudiced than ever against things of a spiritual nature.

Thus I did not a little towards ruining this once

happy family, for even *this* world. At any rate, their happiness is much less than it once was; and there is good reason to fear that I am a prominent cause. But, O the evil I have probably done them for the life to come! I tremble to think of it, and to think that I am now removed in such a manner and to such a distance, that all hope (or nearly all,) of undoing the evil I have done them is at an end. I can pray for them, it is true—but when this is done, I can only commend them to their and my most merciful Father. Some of them are pious people, I believe; but it is in spite of my influence.

It may naturally excite surprise, that the evil results of my doctrines to others, did not create doubts of their correctness. Suspicions that all was not right, did indeed sometimes arise; but a conviction that I was sincere[*] in my purposes and intentions towards mankind, and was seeking to promote their happiness, partially suppressed them. However, I might still have been checked in my career, had it not been for a series of events that will be related in the next chapter.

---

[*] The doctrine that we cannot be materially wrong, if we are only sincere, I must say again, is one of the most dangerous doctrines in the christian world, and ought long ago to have been exploded.

CHAPTER XII.

MY SELF-ESTEEM.

Method of hearing sermons.—Reading books.—Writing a Commentary on the Bible.—An approach to blasphemy.—My creed.

But as I have already intimated, these misgivings were occasional and transient. I believed I had entered on a noble career of improvement. "All persons, places and circumstances," I said in a letter to a friend, "have become my teachers; and every occurrence affords me a lesson." And I may truly say—what has been already intimated—that during no period of my life have I made more *merely* intellectual progress in a given time, than at this period. I will not undertake to say—using the language of phrenologists—how rapidly the *organ of self-esteem* was developing all this while. A few facts, however, will perhaps enable the reader to form an opinion.

I was fond of uttering paradoxes, especially religious ones; such as, "We should be both wholly disinterested and wholly selfish." "There is no such thing as self-denial; the whole business of life is pleasure"—"He that thinks most of earth, thinks most of heaven"—"He that loves himself most, loves God most."—"Enemies are our greatest friends," &c.

Throwing out expressions like these, may seem too trifling to mention in this place, but my object is to show how much pains I took to show my own wisdom, and introduce moral topics for conversation. For in defining the word *pleasure*, for example, in one of the above paradoxes, I gave it such a definition that no one would object to it. By pleasure I meant the highest happiness of the soul, present and prospective.

I was peculiarly fond of hearing discourses and reading books, which supported sentiments wholly contrary to my own; for it afforded me much gratification to refute them, mentally—sometimes in notes with my pencil. I always fancied that I could prove my own sentiments from the very sermons and books which contained the strongest arguments against them. Hearing a sermon, one day, on the eternity of future punishment, I could not help thinking and remarking, that I could prove the contrary doctrine from the minister's own concessions.

A gentleman sent me "Fuller's Calvinism and Socinianism compared." I read it with great attention, and wrote down my objections to his views. They were numerous, but not very important, except one. I took the ground—and thought I established it beyond the possibility of debate—that the whole work was erroneous, because the writer had *begged the question* in the outset. I never saw any thing more clearly, as I then thought, than this. And yet I have lately been surprised, on looking over the work, to find how differently it appears from what it formerly did; and have thus found another proof that "what we ardently wish we soon believe." In truth, I scarcely read a book on any subject, at that period, without finding that it confirmed me in my religious sentiments.

But the scriptures, more than all other books, to me appeared on my side of the question. How differently, thought I, do they appear, and how much more interesting, to those who have learned to study them properly and rationally! I had acquired the art of interpreting almost every thing in such a manner that it gave support to my favorite opinions; and when I found difficulty with a passage, I only concluded that the writer might be under a little mistake. So confident was I of the support which these writings gave to what I called rational or liberal views, that I began to think of writing a commentary on them—not so long as Scott's, but far better, and more free from bigotry! A series of circumstances, however, prevented it; for which I have great cause of thankfulness.

A person wrote to me about this time—it was one of the "new light" men—in regard to a strange propensity among men to magnify Christ, and render him an object of worship, "Why," says he, "I can in almost or quite every instance adopt his language—and in the utmost sincerity too." And though a little startled at first, I thought upon reflection, I could do the same. "My meat and drink," I said to myself, are "to do the will of Him that sent me, and to finish his work." "I came down from heaven, not to do mine own will, but the will of Him that sent me." "I have meat to eat that ye (my poor bigoted brethren) know nothing of." "He that hath seen me, hath seen the Father." "Believest thou not that I am in the Father, and the Father in me?" "He that heareth my words and believeth them, hath everlasting life."—But I forbear; for it seems almost blasphemous to relate it.

What, indeed, but the most consummate vanity

should have induced me and my correspondent to think that we could appropriate to ourselves such declarations? What indeed but the object which we had in view, viz. to bring down the Savior of men from that height which it is perfectly obvious to plain, unprejudiced, unsophisticated common sense he claimed, even from the bosom of the Father in heaven, to the character of a mere dweller upon earth, a frail and fallible being like ourselves—and at the same time, be it observed, to elevate ourselves, in a corresponding degree, above the majority of our fellow men! As to the miracles which Jesus wrought, or the miraculous commencement and termination of his earthly career, we said but little. It was however understood that there was a way of getting over this difficulty; either by referring it to charlatanry, or the mistake or misapprehension of the witnesses, or of the inspired writers.

After having led the reader through a long and no doubt painful maze—a forty year's journey, as it were, in error, I am now approaching a highly important,—and to me, interesting part of my history. And I cannot but think those who have followed me thus far, will have patience to go through with my narrative. But as I have already intimated that I had a creed at this time, and that I could so interpret Scripture as to appear to believe with any, all, or none of my fellow men—just as suited my humor or convenience—it may be best, before proceeding to relate the circumstances that led me out of the path of error, to state as briefly as possible what the leading articles of my creed were.

I believed that there was a *Great First Cause* of the Universe and its inhabitants, and that this First Cause was *good* as well as great. I believed that man, whether he *originated from an oyster* or not, was destined to a glorious immortality; that is, such is the destination of the species, taken as a whole. But whether we were to live again in Jupiter, Herschel, the Sun, or in some remoter part of the universe, to go on forever in the career of perfectibility and immortality, or whether the only immortality to which we were destined, was that of the species collectively considered, and obtainable *alone* on this earth, I was not quite certain.

This earth I conceived to be a great temple for the worship of Jehovah; the facts contained in the book of nature, the principal revelation; and all those employments which had a tendency to promote the happiness of mankind, religious worship. Every day I regarded as the Sabbath; every hour, holy time. Those who ate and drank as they ought, daily held communion with Christ, and with God. Those who lived and moved and breathed only to promote the happiness of mankind, *prayed without ceasing.*

I believed in the Scriptures of the Old and New Testament so far as to believe that they contained many important facts; and whenever I found doctrines there which corresponded with our experience, I admitted them to be the word of God. *Wherever in the universe, there was good*, there, I believed was *God*, whether in this world or elsewhere; and wherever evil was found, there was the grand adversary. I believed that in proportion as we were perfect, morally and religiously, we were adjudged to everlasting life (and this daily and hourly; conscience being the judge on the throne, with the books opened, &c.); and in proportion as our characters were the contrary of all this, we were sentenced to everlasting or *spiritual* (mental) punishment.

I may also add, in this place, before proceeding further, that I thought my faith, in some measure, *tested*, about this time, by the following circumstance. An epidemic disease prevailed, which was very fatal, and I was seized among the rest.

The circumstances and symptoms were such as to threaten danger. But my skeptical faith was strong. Before I became much weakened by disease, I called for pen and paper, and had them placed by my bedside. Then, with considerable effort, I wrote a few lines respecting the disposal of my wordly concerns, together with a few general remarks tending to show, or at least to make others believe that I was at peace with myself, and not only satisfied with my past course but desirous of going on with my efforts to do good, as I called them, in the next world; after which I submitted pretty cheerfully to my fate.* I will not

---

* The following are the closing paragraphs of this singular document, which has been preserved, as a curiosity, to this time. Observe, if you please, how I had religion and religious truths on my tongue, while hanging over the very verge as it were of eternity; and observe too, the curious mixture of truth and error.

"I write this under the impression that I shall not recover; but of this I cannot be certain, of course. If I get well, I shall be glad of it, and shall try to pursue the plan of life I have for some time had marked out. If I die, why perhaps I may have an opportunity to carry on my benevolent plans in some other world.

"Remember it is my anxious request that no formal prayers, sermons, hymns, or any other religious services be permitted near me, during my last days or hours—at house, church, or grave yard. When you have kept my body as

say that there were *no misgivings*; for there were. But I knew that any anxiety in regard to the future would diminish my chance of recovery,—and I also believed that I could not, at the worst, be *very* miserable in any future world. Besides, it was my duty* to die—if die I must—like a man and a philosopher.

Contrary to my expectations, however, I finally recovered. This experiment has strengthened the conviction in my own mind, that people generally die much as they live; and *that the manner of our exit is a miserable test of our religious character;—the public sentiment to the contrary notwithstanding.*

---

long as you think proper, commit it to the grave, in a plain manner, and with as little ceremony as possible.—I am sure you will comply with my request when you know my reasons; one of which is a belief that the cause of truth has always suffered, and always will suffer from connecting ideas of sickness, death, &c., with so many of our religious services. I am determined, with your permission, to set the world a rational example."

* This word *duty*, in every body's mouth who wishes to sustain a good character in society, is particularly so in the mouths of hypocrites and double dealers.

CHAPTER XIII.

MY FURTHER PROGRESS.

The secret getting out.—How I was treated.—Charges against me.—An injudicious minister.—Word of caution.—Publicly reported that I was a Unitarian.—The consequences.

IT was now pretty well understood that I had adopted sentiments which were hostile to evangelical truth. Some thought I was simply a Universalist; some a Unitarian; some who knew that I read the writings of skeptics had strong suspicions of a tendency to infidelity. But instead of coming to me and endeavoring to set me right, they generally took a course which, though meant to put the unwary on their guard, only had the effect to drive me farther and farther from the truth. This was by shrugging the shoulders, shaking the head, sighing, &c., when I happened to be the subject of conversation; adding strong expressions of regret.

One man in particular, who was one of the

best friends I had, after speaking at every convenient opportunity in the most exalted terms of many traits of my character, generally ended with a deep sigh, and the following language, uttered in the most dismal tones conceivable;—"But—I fear he is a long way from the truth."

There was one class of men, (the clergy) it is true, who did not fail to come to me *privately*, and sometimes in a truly christian spirit. They however occasionally fell into such a dictatorial attitude and manner as left me in disgust. The two points on which they assumed that I was radically defective were in regard to the great doctrines of *human depravity* and the *plenary inspiration* of the Scriptures. I was not openly charged with rejecting the Trinity, and had the charge been made, I should have evaded it by equivocal language, as I had not yet acquired courage enough to avow publicly my real sentiments on this point; but I did not hesitate boldly and unequivocally to deny the two former charges. Our discussions, however, usually terminated about where they commenced; only I became more and more disgusted with the dictatorial manner in which I fancied myself treated. I was unwilling to be addressed at the close of an interview with "Well, I hope God will set you right," for it seemed like being treated as an inferior; yet I scorned to reply in the same language.

One of these gentlemen, however was peculiarly unfortunate in his manner of addressing me. He was nearly a stranger in the place, and I think it was only the second time I met with him that he accosted me as follows, almost without any previous compliment;—"My dear sir, why don't you take a decided stand in favor of religion? What a pity your influence should be lost, in a place where it is so much needed."

This was a mode of salutation I did not expect, and I was so much surprised that I said but little in reply. I only assured him that I thought my influence so far as I had influence at all, was by no means *lost* to the cause of religion.

He did not, at that time, accuse me of heresy. But a few days afterwards he called at my room. When he knocked, I was writing, and my manuscript lay spread open as he entered. After a few common-place remarks; "You have something there," said he, "which looks almost like a sermon;"—at the same time begging to know what it was. I told him I was putting down a few thoughts on intemperance.

He asked me to read a few lines. I complied with his request, and read a few pages. I could not help wondering, however, what could be the meaning of such a request, from a man professing to be sane. But my anxiety was soon relieved, for he inquired whether I had ever been in the habit of writing on the subject of *religion ;* and when I answered in the negative, he urged me to write on some particular subject. " I will venture" said he, " to suggest a topic. Suppose you write on *conversion.*"

I told him I could not promise that I would; *perhaps* I might. " But," said he, " if you were going to take up the subject, how would you proceed." I assured him that I was so little accustomed to putting my thoughts together on the subject of religion, that I could not answer him without reflection. He repeated the request that I would write on the subject; observing that Dr. Chalmers, of Scotland, was converted from Socinianism to the truth, while writing the article "Christianity" for the Edinburgh Encyclopedia. Having failed to draw me into free conversation, he at length left me.

A few days afterwards, I met him again at his boarding house. Here we entered into a short discussion on the inspiration of the scriptures. He took the usual evangelical ground, while I maintained that the books of the Old and New

Testament were not, and *could* not be any thing more than the record of a revelation. I do not think I was very successful in defending my position; but the dispute brought me no nearer what I now conceive to be the truth. On the contrary, I was only the more strongly prejudiced against the cause which the minister was advocating. Should this meet the eye of any minister of the gospel, I hope he will learn the necessity—if he is yet in his ignorance—of treating these fastidious folks with more caution. "Wise as serpents and harmless as doves," should be the ministers' motto.

But the secret was now out. It was confidently reported, and to a considerable extent believed, not only at home, but in adjoining towns, that I was a Unitarian. I strenuously denied that I was a Unitarian in any proper sense of the term, but only an *inquirer*. I maintained that I did not believe precisely with any sect whatever, and yet admitted and believed the principal tenets of all. This was indeed more than *half* true; and yet my distant friends and acquaintances in the land of Unitarianism, claimed me as a convert, and I did not undeceive them.

My reasons for this were various. One was a consciousness that I had in some respects already *passed beyond Unitarianism*, and entered the confines of Rationalism or Deism. I knew that if I was persecuted for Unitarianism there was a city of refuge to flee to; but if I became suspected of Deism, or Skepticism, the case was a doubtful one. On this point I was not disappointed; for I learned about this time that "liberal" Christians were as exclusive as other sects, to those who went beyond a certain boundary; and this boundary, said an individual on whom I could rely, "Channing must settle." It was therefore my opinion, as well as that of others, that for the present, Unitarianism was a safe resting place.

My efforts at making converts were by no means remitted. Day and night I devoted my spare moments, either in thought, word, or deed, to the "cause." How much might Christians effect if they were half as active as some of the "enlightened deists" of our country! A few are so, I well know; but taken as a body, I know of no class of citizens at the present day, notwithstanding all the noise which prevails, who are making as much sacrifice according to their means, as some of the disciples of "free inquiry" now are, and for some time have been. On this point I do not speak unadvisedly; for I know where I stand, and to what documents I have had access.

I have said that I made great efforts to procure converts. To one of my correspondents I had already announced the names of several whom I considered as *certain*; one or two of whom had been subjects of the late "revival." Several more I regarded as *thinking*. Any individual who would find fault with orthodoxy—or rather with its abuses, I regarded as more than half converted; for I always felt sure of gradually bringing him to the "truth," as I called it, if I could bring him to censure the existing order of things. At that time I had not fully learned by dear bought experience, as I have since, that it is one thing to "pull down," but quite another affair to "build up." Nor had I fully learned another lesson of at least equal importance, viz., that conviction is not always followed by conversion.

CHAPTER XIV.

MY PROGRESS, CONTINUED.

Specimen of my manner of preaching.—Its effects on Mr. H.—Its general effects.—What is most discouraging about it.

How have I been the dupe of delusive appearances, especially with the middle aged! Many a man of forty-five or fifty years of age has, in the progress of several different conversations, seemed to assent to every thing I could wish; and yet in a little time he would be precisely where he was before. As if his brain was *elastic*, the impressions made on the yielding mass, like those on India rubber, have in a short time entirely disappeared.

The topics I used generally to dwell upon, as an entering wedge to my system, were our public plans for religious and moral improvement. Missionary, Bible, and Temperance societies, and Sunday School Unions were especial objects of my dislike, and against these I found it easy to excite prejudice. Indeed all "associations and combinations of men," (churches, I suppose, were not excepted,) to say the least, were regarded as of doubtful tendency.

One interview in particular, I remember; and this will serve as a specimen. I fell into conversation with Mr. H., a man about fifty, as he rested on the handle of his hoe a few moments to hear and approve my "preaching."

The mind of Mr. H. was filled with fears about what he called an aspiring priesthood; consequently I knew what subject would be most likely to interest him. I said to him; "A mighty effort is now making by the orthodox clergy in this country to secure to themselves an ascendancy in the minds of the community, and this under cover of a pretence to exert a moral influence. An *enlightened* moral influence, might, as a nation, save us; but a moral influence which is unenlightened, would prove, as it ever has done, a curse to society. The genius of this government allows much civil freedom, and this strongly disposes men for *religious* freedom. This our ecclesiastical leaders well know, and govern themselves accordingly. But how? Why, by arraying themselves against mental freedom; and establishing a union between *church and state;* or what is, to all intents and purposes, the same thing.

" I know they all deny that they wish for any such union, but of what use is it to deny a fact so palpable? There can be no doubt in the mind of any reasonable, thinking person, that the orthodox sects in this country are even now combined to obtain an ascendancy over other sects and individuals whom they deem heterodox. Orthodoxy is to be the order of the day—in other words, the established religion;—and he who is not orthodox may get a civil appointment, or sustain himself in an occupation or profession, if he can. And what is this but a union of civil and ecclesiastical power, or a union of church and state?

" Take, for example, the Bible society. The avowed object of this society is to give the Bible to all the earth. First, its various members are to supply their own vicinity,—town, county, state, &c., then, when this is accomplished, they are to go further, and give it to all other nations in their own language. Now, this plan looks very fair. We will take it for granted that the object can be accomplished, and that, if accomplished, it will be beneficial. But it will certainly operate as a monopoly of the sale of books; and monopolies, you and I both abhor.

"Suppose the general depository for the state of New York to be in the city of New York. One depository and one agent,—with, perhaps a few sub-agents—will be sufficient for that great city; but what are fifty or a hundred other booksellers to do? The Society will have such an extensive sale at their command that they can well afford to sell cheaper than other merchants; and this will operate as a complete monopoly, so far as Bibles and Testaments are concerned.

"Do you say that other booksellers will still have the sale of other books? To be sure they may; but who can doubt that the Sunday School Union will soon make the same persons and places the agents and depositories for the sale of all Sabbath school books? Next, all public libraries must be supplied from the same source; then all other school books must come from this particular quarter; and thus the whole book trade will, by degrees, be turned into the same channel.

"You may say to me, 'Where is the harm of all this, since we have at present far too many men engaged in the business, and on your own supposition a smaller number of men will be employed, but they will be *better* men, and jockies will be discouraged; besides which, books of a given quality will be much *cheaper* than they are at present.'

"But suppose the same sects should go further (and who can doubt that they will?) and form a tea, a tobacco, or a sugar society, and monopolize the whole trade in those articles, would public opinion tolerate it? Yet we cannot doubt that those articles would be cheaper, if not of better quality, than they now are. Yet we quietly permit the American Bible Society to monopolize the sale of Bibles; and when this shall be effected, what is to hinder them from extending the monopoly to other books, to tea, sugar, and *every things else in the market?*

"Now who does not see that all power would thus eventually be thrown into the hands of those sects, and individuals of this country, who now monopolize to themselves the name of orthodox? The depositories for *every* thing will then be in the hands of such men as their leaders shall choose to appoint; that is, of some one of their favored sects, or perhaps, finally, the members exclusively of some of their favorite churches. In those days, wo be to him who does not become orthodox, and join an orthodox church. Happy may he consider himself in obtaining a place, as a hewer of stones or a drawer of water to those in authority and power.

"If this would not be a union of church and state—and with a vengeance too—I beg to know what would. The charge is supposed to be repelled by asserting that no sect in the land aims thus at usurping the throne of public sentiment. This is true; no *one* sect does. But a union of the strongest and most numerous sects can do it, and will do it too, unless the world awake from their lethargy. But are the free people of United America prepared to submit their rights to ecclesiastical tyranny without a struggle? Though already shorn of some of the locks of their power, will they not make one mighty effort; and if they cannot shake off the chains which already begin to bind them, will they not at least,—like Samson among the Philistines—die an *honorable death?*

"Almost all the benevolent societies with which this country abounds, are so connected at present, as to constitute parts for uniting this great system of church and state. Such is the fact at least in relation to the Conference and Revival system, the Foreign and Domestic Missionary Associations, Sabbath School Unions, Temperance Societies, &c.; and there is very little doubt that the Lyceum system is going the same way. Not that all the individuals who are members of these associations have in view this union of civil and ecclesiastical affairs, but their leaders undoubtedly have."

This harangue so nearly fell in with Mr. H.'s views that he was not a little gratified to listen to a discourse of half an hour's length. My object in presenting it to the reader is to show him, if he is not already familiar with the fact, what sort of views—however destitute of *argument* or truth they may be—are studiously, industriously, and successfully propagated in our country. I say successfully too, for I never yet failed to secure the attention, and seldom, to win the hearts of a certain class of the community, when I presented them. It is true their specious appearance was often seen through by men of as much intelligence as Mr. H.: and yet some of even such persons will listen.

The worst difficulty the apostles of these sentiments have to encounter is, that their disciples, when actually *obtained*, are good for nothing. They cannot be relied on. They are easily driven about by every wind of doctrine that prevails. The bias of their hearts being wrong, they drink in with greediness all manner of revolutionary opinions; and, perhaps, were a mob ready to pull down or burn some meeting house, under cover of midnight darkness, they would join them against "*church and state.*" But only let half a dozen of the sun's rays break in upon them, and they shrink to their quarters, and cower to public opinion.

When I used to have a gaping crowd,—perhaps at some tippling house—hearing my suggestions, as if for their lives, I sometimes caught the spirit of an "apostle of free inquiry," and thought for the moment I would go forth a missionary in the cause. And I have no doubt that such missionaries would be successful in gathering hearers from lanes, hedges, and ditches. But suppose you collect an army of these people to join in a crusade against church and state; what then? True, you get here and there a man of some force—perhaps about enough for ringleaders, not more—but the mass, what are they? Alas! I know too well. I have spent too much of my breath on such "dry bones," not to know that one disciple of common sense and real principle will chase an army of a thousand of them—and two put to flight *ten* thousand.

CHAPTER XV.

TOUR OF OBSERVATION.

Encouraging circumstances among the Universalists.—Commenced a tour of observation.—Faces of my audiences.—Unitarian preaching and practice.—Meeting with singular individuals.—On the point of going over to the Free Inquirers.—What prevented me.—Re-examined the evidences in favor of a Revelation.

HITHERTO I had enjoyed no opportunity of hearing Unitarian preaching, or of observing the habits and general character of those who were openly the adherents of this system. With the Universalists I was much better acquainted. I ad generally found them a moral people externally, and had lived in the family of one who used to call his household together every Sunday morning, to read, in their hearing, a chapter in the Bible. I found them also favorably disposed towards the Unitarians, and not strongly "prejudiced" against those who were more "liberal." Some of them would read the writings of her who was regarded as the *female Apostle* of those sentiments,—I mean Fanny Wright—and not a few secretly approved them; though they were ostensibly opposed to skepticism. I could not, however, avoid entertaining great hope that this sect might, without much difficulty, be " emancipated." It was not difficult to make them reject the doctrine of the " trinity " and the " plenary inspiration of the scriptures; " and when this was done, I believed (and justly,) an individual or sect to be on the high road to Robert Owen and Fanny Wright's land of mental and moral " independence."

But I was determined to know something of Unitarianism in practice—if not of skepticism; so, partly for this purpose, and partly for other objects, I commenced a tour of observation.

The first thing which I discovered worth mentioning, was, the ease with which I could every where collect a circle to hear me declaim against bigotry, and superstition, and mystery, and sectarianism. Keeping names out of sight, I found no difficulty in presenting, gradually and cautiously, nearly all the " liberal " doctrines of Channing, Dewey, and Follen; and not a few of those which I regarded as a step in advance of theirs. Wherever I went, I found the state of things the same. The great stumbling block in the way of my progress abroad as well as at home, was, the character of those who composed the audience where I held forth. There were often too many red faces and bottle noses to please a friend of total abstinence from extra stimulants.

The first Unitarian preacher whom I had the pleasure of hearing—and who, by the way, was a most excellent man in point of mere common morality, and a would-be philanthropist—appeared to me to be involved in a contradiction. He took advantage of the usual orthodox concession, that Christ was a *man ;* and then, in another part of his discourse, attempted to show, by way of defence against the charge of Humanitarianism, that he was *more* than man. **What** he was considered to be besides a man, I did not learn ; and do not know to this day. To say that he was divinely commissioned, explains nothing ; for Moses and Paul, without being any thing but men, were divinely commissioned. Besides, to suppose the human nature united to some other *created* nature, requires, as it appears to me, stronger faith and greater credence in **mystery** than the doctrine of a peculiar, though **mysterious,** Divine nature, and the union of this nature for a short time with the human.

Another thing which perplexed me was, the fact that in some of our cities, the Unitarians were among the fashionable and the gay. To me, unaccustomed as I was to much of the display of fashionable life, this was shocking. Still I could not help secretly approving it. "This," thought I, "is but the other extreme; and men are prone to extremes. They have been accustomed to a *long faced, monkish religion*; and in leaving it, nothing is more natural than that they should go to the other extreme. They will come round right after a while. *Things always regulate themselves.*"

Unitarians profess to be above the proselyting spirit; and I think generally are so. Still, should this meet the eye of any one of them who seeks to bring his fellow men—by influence—to what he deems a better faith than the "Orthodox," he will do well to devise a lesson from the foregoing. Few men, however vicious they are themselves—however given to levity, luxury, extravagance, foppery, or even gluttony and intemperance, approve it in others. And it will be found that many of the practices in which Unitarians are known to indulge have been hitherto an obstacle in the way of the dissemination of their principles. To make Unitarians *faster* than they now do, if this be an object with them, as with some, it most undoubtedly is, they must become much more Orthodox—I mean in their practice—than they now are.

Let it be remembered that I speak generally; for though there are exceptions to the truth of these remarks, they are not very numerous. The same class of persons who set luxurious tables, who indulge in extravagance in dress, equipage, and a thousand other things; and who attend late evening parties, balls and theatres, and occasionally play a game at whist, would, were they in England or Spain, enter into the *more refined sports,* such as fox-hunting, bull baiting, &c.; and with equal salaries play the same unchristian game throughout, which is played by so many of the English priests and bishops.

With the exception I have just made, and *one more*, I was generally much pleased with liberalism and with " liberal " preaching. The latter was well calculated, as I thought, to prepare the way for a better and a more liberal state of things. I did not think the clergy were going too fast; but, on the whole, just about fast enough for the general good; as fast as human nature—abused as it had been—could well bear.

The second difficulty I met with in regard to

their doctrines as they were set forth,—a difficulty to which I have just alluded,—was the following.

A preacher of Philadelphia inculcated the notion that there was such a thing as real disinterestedness, and that it was a christian duty to aspire to it. This was laying the axe at the root of my system. Besides, I thought it was equally fatal to "liberal" christianity. I cannot conceive even now, how it is possible for any thinking person to put the two things together. Nay, I am certain that what I call disinterested benevolence can never harmonize either with Unitarianism or skepticism. They both require an admission of the doctrine of supreme selfishness—not a *low* selfishness, it is true—but an enlarged and liberal one; the doing of every thing with a reference to our own happiness, either more or less extended.

Not far from this time, I met with a young candidate for the ministry, who was about to be installed in a very respectable "liberal" society; and ascertaining that he was familiar with the writings of Hume, Godwin, and others of the same stamp, I ventured to introduce conversation on the subjects of which they treat; and ultimately on the writings of Paul. In the progress of the conversation, I asserted that the apostle Paul's reasoning was evidently sometimes quite *inconclu-*

sive. "I do not think," said he, with a significant look and tone, "that we are driven to the necessity of *saying* quite so much."

This struck me forcibly, for it appeared like a silent admission of the truth of my position; a thing which I had not expected.

But a more *startling* circumstance, occured sometime after this. In conversation with a person in one of our cities who was nominally a Unitarian, and whose amiable character, and unexceptionable moral excellence, not to say philanthropy, had secured the entire confidence of some of the first men of that sect, and, indeed of all who knew him, the influence of the Bible, as it is generally understood, received, and used, was mentioned as being an obstacle in the way of human improvement. Mankind must always be children, he thought, so long as such a blind submission was paid to *that book*, and he was anxious to see its authority *tumbled* down.*

His language was so impassioned, and his man-

---

* He meant no doubt, the *kind* of authority which it usually maintains. If science or experience had already demonstated the truth of a thing which he found there, he was evidently ready to receive it; for it was then rational. But what is the use of the Bible, if it be but to confirm what we already know?

ner so earnest, that while it left not a doubt in my mind of his *sincerity*, it convinced me of a bitterness against the usual manner of receiving and regarding the Bible, which I did not expect; and though I had long inclined to the sentiment myself, it struck me with a kind of horror to hear it avowed by another, from which I have not entirely recovered to this hour. Whenever I recollect the circumstance I fancy I see him with a frowning countenance, and in a mixed emotion of pity and rage, denouncing the very book whose authority Voltaire hated, and was equally anxious to destory.

But it affords me some consolation to know that the individual to whom I refer, now views the subject in a different light, and reflects with pain on his feelings and views at that period of what he calls his moral progress. I do not say that he has yet become a humble, child-like follower of the Savior; but he is very far indeed from being a disciple of Voltaire. And it is not delegated to me to say to what depths of error in sentiment a person may descend without getting beyond the reach of that mercy which is in a sense unlimited.

In another instance and in another place, I fell in with a gentleman of a character equally unexceptionable, and who passed equally well for a Unitarian. This gentleman, after considerable conversation, was found to entertain sentiments somewhat similar to the other. Finding that he was fond of conversing on the subject, I had become rather bold, and had objected to the character of Christ, when viewed as a perfect example; and he had at first assumed an attitude of defence. But his defence was of that loose kind which only confirmed me in the belief that he was a skeptic. For when I proposed difficulties in the way of receiving the Christian faith, he only gave what he said *might* be a reply to my objections. In no case did he use the indicative mode of speech, but always the potential.

I now for the first time made known to one or two persons in whom I thought I could confide, a resolution I had half formed, of going over, at once, to the "Free Inquirers" or "Skeptics." As to a written revelation, I had lost all confidence in it and its adherents; though I still abhorred many of the opinions of the skeptics. Their rough and offensive manner of presenting and defending them, was also equally odious. But the thought of the pain my apostacy would give to my friends, together with other considerations somewhat trying, kept me from making shipwreck.

The advice of liberal friends was now sought. One advised me to visit the "Free Inquirers," and ascertain what my prospects would be if I joined them. Another *would not advise me*, but said that if I should determine on such a course, he knew of a desirable *situation* among them, in one of our principal cities, which it was possible I might obtain.* But I still hesitated.†

Meanwhile, I fell in with one or two individuals who had entered deeply into several subjects which formerly occupied my attention, and with whom I could sympathize; but whose religious views were wholly "orthodox." I was surprised to find our *general* notions of things correspond, when on a single topic we differed so widely; for it appeared to me as strange that the various opinions held by these persons could harmonize, as that light should harmonize with darkness.

It is probable that this meeting with the individual referred to, saved me from making the desperate decision. For some time after this, however, I stood on the verge of skepticism, not

---

* This situation was ultimately secured to a gentleman and lady who were true disciples of Kneeland. The school, however, was not permanently flourishing. The lady is said to have recently become a believer.

† See Appendix, note D.

knowing whether to go backward or forward. I was becoming utterly sick, however, of Unitarianism. I viewed it as an inefficient "milk and water" system. Besides, I was confident no rational, consistent, and inquiring mind, that had once adopted "liberal" principles, could fail of coming to the ground I then occupied—that there was no defensible middle ground between orthodoxy and downright skepticism. To one of them I felt I must go ultimately—yea soon—but, to which? This I could not determine. *Orthodoxy*, I could not believe, nor even the Christian religion;— Skepticism I was a little afraid of.

At length I determined to make a tour of discovery among the "free inquirers," and ascertain what my propects of usefulness would be among them; and who, if I joined them, were likely to be my *associates*. I found they had greatly overrated their numbers, talents, and respectability; though not their zeal or disposition to make proselytes. Indeed, I was confirmed in the opinion that no class of citizens were laboring harder or making greater sacrifices to accomplish their purposes, than they.

Still I did not quite like their appearance. It was not very gratifying, after hearing a lecture on chemistry on the Sabbath, to witness at the close a scene of amusement with the nitrous oxyd or exhilarating gas. I returned to my home, and for some time continued in a state of painful suspense.

About this period, a work of Dr. Chalmers, of Scotland, was handed me. As I knew something of the Doctor's history, and that he had been, during his early life, for many years a Socinian, I took hold of the work, and read it with much interest. This was followed by a re-examination of Paley's Evidences of Christianity. These works—especially that of Chalmers;—made some impression; and I began to think that religion, after all, *might be true.*

As to the argument which is sometimes urged, that it is *safer* to believe, than to disbelieve, because if religion should prove true, we are then safe, but if untrue, we are yet as safe as others; I most heartily despised it, and still do. The same train of argument is sometimes urged in behalf of the doctrine of eternal punishment; but it does appear to me, we ought to be ashamed of it. I am wholly opposed to such arguments in any case; but in religion above all, they are abominable. If religion is true, let it be received—if not, reject it. So of the doctrine of future punishment, or any other doctrine. Heaven is, or should be, something more than a place of mere escape from hell, or a receptacle of hypocrites;—it is a *positive* state, or it does not and ought not to exist.

The arguments of Dr. Chalmers at length appeared so convincing, that I found it more difficult to resist the weight of evidence in favor of christianity, than to receive it. On any other subject, when the arguments in favor of the thing were, for example, as twenty, and those against it only nineteen, if I thought I had made a thorough investigation of the whole subject, and the time had arrived when it was my duty to act, I knew I should yield at once to the preponderating evidence. Why then should I not yield in the present case? I found, at length, that I must do so, or give up all claim to common sense. As a choice of difficulties, then, Revelation was received.

CHAPTER XVI.

SPECULATIVE INQUIRIES.

Revelation being admitted, new difficulties arise about some of its doctrines.—The divine nature.—My inquiries.—Dr. Channing's notions of the dignity of human nature.—The views of evangelical sects on this subject.

But I now found difficulties thickening upon me on every side. If a revelation had been made by God, I was bound to ascertain what it taught. Hitherto, I had supposed that the question lay between skepticism and orthodox or evangelical sentiments; and that in rejecting the one, I could not avoid going at once with my whole heart to the other. How was I disappointed! Though compelled to admit a divine revelation, my heart rose against every leading orthodox doctrine; and I seemed further from peace of mind and self-satisfaction than before. Though I had been disgusted with Unitarianism in practice, the whole array of what I had been accustomed at one period to regard as scriptural argument in its favor now presented itself before me. In short, I found myself obliged to return by the way I came; and to retrace almost every step of my wanderings.

My first conflict was with the doctrine of the Trinity. This was a great mystery. Must I admit, as a fact, a mode of existence so mysterious? Mysteries, at this time, were terrible things to me. *Philosopher*, as I wished to be, I seemed to forget that ten thousand things existed in the world around me, the manner of whose existence was as really a mystery, as the manner of existence of three persons in one God.

A friend, in a walk with me one day, put me upon a new train of thought. Said he, "you are fond of making man a kind of *triune*, composed of body, mind, and heart; but do you comprehend the nature of this triple union? If you do not, why should you speak of them so frequently, as if they were in some measure independent of each other, when they really constitute but one individual?" I could not answer him.

My friend's remark was just; for I was then, and am still, exceedingly partial to this view of the nature of man. It appears to me to accord entirely with every known fact in regard to our wonderful and wonderfully complicated character; as well as with the declaration of revelation concerning it. Even Phrenology, which has of late excited so much attention, recognizes, most decidedly, this triple nature. "Every man knows himself," says a phrenologist of some eminence, "to be an animal being, an intellectual being, and a moral being; yet no man can tell *how* these exist distinctly yet unitedly in his single self; while yet he is conscious that they do thus exist." So I used to say, without knowing or caring much about Phrenology. And so I still say. And hence too I found no difficulty in receiving upon testimony so ample, the great doctrine of the triune nature of the Deity. Indeed I could not else see how man was made in his image.

But the statements of the record—how were they to be met? Jesus there represents himself as inferior to the Father. True, but he also represents himself as *one* with the Father; as being Alpha and Omega, the first and the last, the beginning and the ending—the Almighty. Others call him God, the Creator, the mighty God, the everlasting Father, &c. Now if we assume that he was truly God, the expressions which imply inferiority can be accounted for, on the ground of his being a mediator, &c.; but if we assume that he was a derived, dependent being, how can we account for the frequent application of titles to him which can belong only to the Supreme God?

There were other considerations. He never said, "Thus saith the Lord," but "*I*" say so or so. This was never done before or since, by any sound-minded being on the earth. Of course, his character was a peculiar one. But if not a *man*, what was he? "*I* will give everlasting life," said he. "*I* will raise him up at the last day." "If ye ask any thing in my name, *I* will give it you." But the authorities on this point are too numerous to quote here. Finally I found myself compelled to admit the doctrine of the Father, Son, and Holy Spirit; were it only as a choice of difficulties.

Let me not be understood as saying or supposing that these are the only, or the best arguments in favor of the views of Trinitarians. I am only speaking of the operations of my own mind at the time; and what the evidence was, which at that time presented itself. At the present moment, I should take a widely different course of reasoning from that which influenced me, and led me to the sentiments which I now entertain, to convince a Unitarian of what I conceive to be his error.

For my own part, at present, I feel not at all

inclined to appeal to what are usually regarded as the direct proofs on this subject. The indirect evidence is quite sufficient, and even strikes me with most force. This indirect evidence is found on almost every page of the New Testament. The manner in which the Savior speaks; the authority he assumes; the right and powers he claims; and the predictions he utters respecting himself, cannot certainly comport with any thing like modesty or even *sanity*, if he were a created being. Assume the point that he was so, and I am compelled to stumble at every step, and become more and more involved in difficulty; but granting him to be God and man—God made flesh and blood and dwelling among us—and though I do not say that all difficulties are removed, yet I do affirm that, to me, the path is comparatively clear, and the New Testament language comparatively intelligible.

Though I had been compelled to admit the doctrine of the Trinity, I had occasional misgivings. Not that the state of the argument appeared to me to vary, but the power of habit was so great, that such trains of skeptical thought and feeling, and such common cavils, would occasionally come up, as for the moment seemed overwhelming.

The thought, "Could the Creator die!" was a leader of one of these associations, and was very troublesome. I had admitted doctrines which appeared to involve such an opinion, but it was a "hard saying;" and after all, I sometimes thought, "may there not be a mistake about it?"

But "what is death?" I used upon reflection to ask myself. "Is it the destruction of any thing? Is there any greater difficulty in believing that the Creator *died*, than that he ate, and drank, and slept? Jesus certainly exercised the functions, and met with temptations common to *man*. Where then the mighty difficulty of supposing that after he had been a man in other respects, and had passed through the changes to which man is subject, he went through the *last* change?"

Sometimes, after a train of reasoning like the foregoing, the clouds would disperse; at others, they would only thicken upon me. There were seasons when I felt as if I must and should go back to skepticism. I felt that I had no *heart* to attend to religion. All my feelings,—all my habits of thinking and reasoning—were so much of the "doubting system," that I thought religion, if true, of no consequence to me; that it must always "play round the head," but never reach "the heart." At seasons I almost thought, with Dr. Payson, that

I could bring such a single argument against the Christian religion, as was alone sufficient to demolish it.*

My only escape from this state of mind was to consider that I had once settled the question according to the best evidence I could obtain, and that I was bound to act upon that decision until more evidence should appear. This consideration commonly afforded relief for a short time; but it sometimes cost me hours of struggling with the current of unbelief, before I could overcome it.

One day I met with an old correspondent of the Unitarian denomination, who had heard with great pain that I was relapsing into what he called the "old school" doctrine. But he treated me with a great deal of gentleness, and only insinuated that I had never understood the Unitarians; that I had viewed the subject partially, or in a distorted form; that there was not the shadow of a doubt that our sentiments were still pretty nearly alike.

"But do you really believe," said he, "that Jesus Christ was God?" "Certainly he was so, *in a sense*," I replied. He said he did not like to hear me say, *in a sense*, for it was evading the question. I had no idea, however, of evasion,

---

* See Appendix, note E.

but I was unwilling to enter into a discussion of the subject at the time; so it was deferred. This circumstance, however, I always regretted. I ought to have stated my belief, in plain terms; and then, if I did not wish to discuss the subject, I could have said so. I had not at this time—if indeed I ever have—learned much of gospel simplicity. I ought to have been the more particular to avoid the least appearance of " dodging " the question, from the fact, that many who entertain erroneous sentiments are much addicted to this unreasonable practice; which is one of many reasons why they continue to hold, with so much pertinacity, their errors. Truth never needs to shun fair and open, and manly discussion.

About this time, I fell in with a biographical sketch of Dr. Godman, of Philadelphia. This gentleman had, in early life, entertained the sentiments of the French school—or in other words, skepticism. A few years before his death he became a humble and an apparently devoted Christian. There was something in his history so much like my own, that it affected me. Besides this, the sentiments he expressed in relation to death, were so rational and philosophical, and at the same time so *Christian*, that they made a deep and abiding impression on my mind.

My former friends, "liberal" as they were, began to give me up as lost. They wondered, indeed, how the apostacy could happen; but concluded, perhaps that I was influenced by some improper considerations. Some of them thought I was afraid of jeopardizing my popularity by remaining on liberal ground; and had turned back to serve a purpose.

They were, however, mistaken. All my hopes in a pecuniary point of view, were on the other side of the question. And had I been seeking for distinction,—nothing would have better suited me than to become a pioneer in the cause of "free inquiry." That cause, I then believed to be in a way to become more popular, *for a short time*, than it had hitherto been. How far my belief was well grounded, the world will soon see, if they have not seen already.

The reason is, that we have not yet learned to oppose its progress in a proper manner. We have zeal enough on the subject, but it is *misdirected*; or spends itself in *words*. The way to *put down* real heresy, is to *put up* the truth;—the way to *put up the truth* is to educate the rising generation on religious—I do not say sectarian—but *religious* principles. They are to be trained, not to be *half* Christians, but *whole* ones; not to rest satisfied with the mere accumulation of property by *thousands*, and the spending of it by *tens*; but we are to go to the whole extent of self-denial and sacrifice—if indeed there is any self-denial about it—and not only *earn* our thousands, but *spend* our thousands. Religion, (such is the arrangement of God) never progressed, in the individual or in the community, any faster than sacrifice was made, either of appetite, pleasure, reputation, property, health, time, talent, or life.

On the whole, however, two points were established; first, that the Bible was the truth of God; and secondly, that Jesus Christ was equal to, and one with the Father. Not but that I had momentary doubts come over my mind, even on these points; yet such was the nature and character of the evidence, that I found myself compelled to assent to it, or give up every claim to consistency and even to honesty. But in every other respect, strange as it may seem, I was really as much a skeptic as ever. In thinking or conversing upon Revelation or the doctrine of the Trinity, I was evangelical in sentiment; but I no sooner stepped aside to consider any other subject in religion or morals, than my mode of thinking and reasoning was wholly changed—and I did not fail to take the usual ground of modern infidels. So thoroughly were all my habits of thinking, and feeling, and reasoning, and acting, formed in the school of skepticism.

I was willing to believe what the Bible should be found to teach, and to receive its doctrines as coming from God. When Christ announced a truth, I was willing to regard it as the voice of the Father. The only question now was, "what does Jesus say?" or, "what does the Bible teach?"

But in ascertaining what was taught, there was still too much of going to the Bible with pre-established theories and prejudices. It had been a favorite maxim with me, that "no person in the world has ever yet *read the Bible*." By this was meant that no person had come to it without prepossessions and prejudices; and that these must of necessity have produced distorted views of truth. So that no one had ever yet found the pure truths actually contained in it. Now it was that I felt the force of this maxim as applied to myself. I was perpetually falling into the error of trying the Bible doctrines by my own opinions. I believed, for example, that there was nothing in human nature, if the proper measures were taken, to prevent a child's being made to do right. But to this end I thought authority must be kept entirely out of sight; and that the great art of governing consisted in knowing how to arrange things and circumstances in such a manner that the child would choose to do precisely what we *wished* to have him do. I regarded every thing like a *command*, as having a tendency to diminish the child's respect for himself, and of course to injure him.

I thought that much, if not all that perversity which we find in the juvenile nature, though developed ever so early, arose from the fact that we *took* children to be perverse; thus forming a perverse second nature *for* them, and then charging it back upon our first parents or elsewhere. Hence in endeavoring to ascertain the Scriptural declarations concerning this subject, I was perpetually liable to wrong conclusions; because (though at the time insensible of it) I first set up my own opinion as a standard, and then endeavored to make the Scriptures conform to that opinion.

I found the more difficulty in regard to the doctrine of human depravity from the fact of having filled my head with Dr. Channing's notions about the dignity of human nature. For although the Orthodox community should be found to have often erred by looking too much on the *dark* side of things, yet I am fully confident *they* are in an error far more dangerous who dwell always on the *bright* side.

The Unitarian view of human nature, and the dignity of that nature, is to the multitude of mankind, like a pleasant tune from one who can play well on an instrument, but it leaves no permanent, or at least useful impression. There may be a few who are roused by it—indeed I am quite *sure* there are; but their number is very small. We live in a world of Scribes and Pharisees,—men who are trained to the form of godliness without the power. On such men, the smooth preaching of our Unitarian friends produces no good results—unless it is beneficial to inflate men with pride, and set them to thanking God that they are not as other men are.

A very different course was pursued by the Founder of christianity. Religion, like rowing against tide, wind and current, was then found to require effort. But now, according to some modern teachers, it consists of little else than gently gliding down a smooth and equable current—not of water, but of oil. Whether the end of the voyage will be prosperous, eternity must decide.

It has always appeared to me a little singular that those who talk about the *dignity* of human nature, should in their dealings with men, be most on their guard against their depravity. There are no persons more forward than they to complain of the *prejudice*, the *ignorance*, the *error*, of certain individuals, and even classes. At one time, their complaints are against one person or class of persons; at another, their denunciations fall elsewhere; and in the end, few escape them. They talk much of their sympathy with the common ranks of men, and the lower walks of life, but with republicanism on their tongues, they are apt to be *aristocratical* in their practice.

Evangelical Christians have as much confidence as others in the dignity of human nature. For while they believe that without the influences of the Holy Spirit, they "can do nothing" which shall be effectual towards working out their own salvation, they yet believe that with such assistance they "can do all things;" can become "perfect," even as their "Father in heaven is perfect." To what greater dignity is it possible to aspire than this? They do not believe, it is true, that there is in every individual a spark of the Divine nature which only requires nourishing and cherishing—and such influences from the Creator as he sheds on the animal and vegetable world—to make it spring up unto everlasting life. They believe that there is an analogy between the modes of operating on the material and spiritual worlds, which the Creator has adopted, *to a certain extent;*—but that beyond this it fails. They believe that we go astray, and discover by our conduct the total absence of any relish for true holiness, from the first, and that nothing but that influence from on high, which may justly be termed supernatural, would ever lead that which is earthly, to aspire after that which is pure and heavenly. We all endeavor to avoid pain and secure pleasure. But the pleasure, or *heaven* which we *naturally* seek, is the creature of our own imagination, and partakes of our own character. This being utterly unholy, the heaven after which we seek, even if we really suppose we seek heaven, being a creature of our own imagination, cannot be holy.

CHAPTER XVII.

MY VIEWS IN MORALS.

Mere morality considered.—Popular mistakes on this subject.—A practical illustration of the difference between morality and religion.

ONE of the last things a man of skeptical turn—and so indeed of every sinner—will relinquish, in coming to Christ is, the hope of securing the favor of God by his own good conduct. He will have it that he is to be rewarded *for* his good works, and not *according* to them, as the Scripture states it. Tell him a person may possess the most excellent moral character that ever was known (I mean in the *usual sense* of the word *moral*) and yet be as far from the kingdom of heaven as the most grossly vicious, and he rejects the statement with disdain.

Indeed this confounding morality with religion appears to me to be one of the most fatal errors of the day. It is not confined to any class of men, but finds its advocates in almost every sect.

With the Unitarians and Universalists, so far as I am acquainted, it is nearly universal.

They say that to be holy is to be like Christ, and that in proportion as we resemble him, we are truly holy, and must consequently be happy. Very well. No one doubts it. But what *is* being *like Christ?* They tell us it is to do no harm, to obey the dictates of conscience, &c. One says, it is " to do justice, to love mercy, and to endeavor to make our fellow creatures happy."

But is this all? It is well as far as it goes; but it is nothing more than yielding obedience to the command, " Thou shalt love thy neighbor as thyself." It happens that there is another command besides this, and it is denominated by Him who gave it, the *first* and *great* one; " Thou shalt love the Lord thy God, with all thy heart, mind, soul, and strength.

Now to be like Christ we must keep his commandments. We must love God. We must have that affection which the Savior so well describes when he says, " Except ye be converted and *become as little children*, ye cannot enter into the kingdom of heaven."

Do we talk about being like Christ, and yet scarcely send up one thought or prayer to heaven? He was *often* in prayer—*earnest* prayer too. Occasionally he even prayed all night. To be like Christ we must not only do no harm and do good, constantly, but we must have a childlike love to God, as well as confidence in Him, and whenever duty requires it, be willing to lay down even our lives for his sake. But with those who talk about mere morality's carrying a man to heaven, repentance, faith, and love, as exercises towards God, with a disposition to deny ourselves, and if required, even yield up our life, are seldom, if ever, taken into the account.

And as to the morality of which they speak, it may exist without one thought of God, or one particle of regard to his command that we should love him. Religion has produced such a state of public opinion that it is reputable to be outwardly moral. Hence many who have always breathed an atmosphere, as it were, of that morality which religion has produced, and have been formed to those virtuous habits, which, originating in the same source have become universally approved, are unexceptionably moral; and the credit is given either to morality, or to the religion of nature. But this is in my view a species of fraud.

Several of the leading Unitarians of this country were trained in orthodox habits, by orthodox friends; and their moral characters are excellent.

Nay, it would not be strange if they should be found to possess much of true christian character in this respect. How indeed could it be otherwise? But what is to become of the *next* generation? Can a generation trained on Unitarian principles become any thing more than pure Deists? It is impossible!

The leaders of the sect may fancy otherwise; but it will be found that they are mistaken. I am fully satisfied that nothing but Orthodox *feelings*, induced by his education, will save a person who takes Unitarian ground from gradually sliding down into Deism, and finally into Skepticism; I mean if he is honest. I do not judge thus, simply because myself and a few others have run this course, but because this is ever the tendency. This is the way the Germans are going. This is the way, sooner or later, many in our own country will go.*

It may be seen from the foregoing views why I believe the mere moralist, however excellent his character, to be as far from the kingdom of heaven,

---

* This paragraph was written many years since. I do not claim to be "a prophet or the son of a prophet;" but it is not difficult to see that what I foretold is already beginning to be fulfilled.

or holiness, as the most vicious character. Indeed I know not how to avoid the conclusion that he must be much farther from it. The better his character—provided he neglect or despise religion—the more dangerous is he as a member of the community, and the greater the number that will stumble over him into a miserable eternity.

For what does he but, in effect, defraud religion by taking from her that which is justly her due, and placing it to the account of morality? Besides, he leads others to neglect religion and trust in mere morality; and his example, in this respect, is influential just in proportion to the elevation of his character.

If, then, religion is indispensable to the civil welfare, why is not that man the most dangerous man—I mean to the community—whose moral character is the best, but who neglects and thus despises real religion?

Let me, by an illustration, show that morality is not religion. Suppose a good father sends his son to perform certain labors during the day, and return at evening. He expects he will behave well, and of course, treat people kindly. The son is about to obey, but something occurs to divert his attention from his father's business. He falls into another mode of employment for the day, which his father did not intend. He is industrious in his occupation, performs his work well; his conduct, in every respect, is so excellent that he is approved by every body, although it was known what his father directed him to do;—and he goes home.

But *does* his father approve? He commanded him to do so and so. The son went about something which he did not intend, and never thought of him during the day. And although he behaved well where he was, yet he practically despised his father's authority, and set a very dangerous example.

So with the mere moralist. God's first command is; "Son, give me thy heart." He goes about a course, perhaps, which secures the highest applause of his fellow citizens, while he disobeys God and draws down upon himself—and justly too—his indignation.

The truly good man should carry along with him, in all the circumstances and conditions of life, a pleasing and comforting sense of God's presence. I do not believe there is any more difficulty in doing so, and yet performing our business, as his servants, faithfully, than there is of a school boy's retaining a sense of the presence of his instructor and yet be able to pursue faithfully his studies. There is a kind of consciousness that the teacher is present, without actually and really thinking of it; and so it may be with the christian in regard to the presence of God.

It was reasoning of this character that led me gradually, to those views of depravity, regeneration, the necessity of the influence of the Holy Spirit, &c., which are usually styled orthodoxy. The simple reading of the Bible, in a manner as unprejudiced as I could, also had its influence. Doubts remained, but they gradually disappeared; and though my heart remained unaffected, my understanding was more and more convinced.

I am now drawing towards a close of my long narrative. Those who have patiently followed me thus far, are hereby assured that I shall soon relieve them.

CHAPTER XVIII.

MY FINAL RECOVERY TO THE TRUTH.

Stupidity of my mind and heart.—Conviction of danger.—Final resolution.—Change of feeling.—Elements of this change.—Improper encouragement.

I HAD acquired, about this time, a healthy appetite. I used no drink but water, and cannot say that I desired any other. It had a far better relish than any stimulating drink formerly had. I had, moreover removed most of the excitants usually taken with our food. In short, I found myself in these respects, for once a free man. Whether this had any thing to do with my escape from error, I cannot say; but the fact should be noticed.

At the same time I had not only become convinced of the general correctness of the religious doctrines commonly called evangelical; but I had also learned that there is such a thing as a belief of the head which does not affect the heart; for it is with the heart alone, that man " believeth unto righteousness." I had, it is true, my hours of doubt; and distressing ones, too, some of them were; but on the whole I assented to christian truth; and though I received it as a choice of difficulties, still I received it.

Things went on thus for some time. I was occasionally reminded by some event of Providence or the inquiry of some anxious or solicitous friend, that all was not right; but the conviction, like the morning dew, soon disappeared. Every reflection on the subject and on my existing state, deepened the impression that my heart was far from being in subjection to the law of God;—that I was, in short, "without hope and without God in the world."

At this time I attended church, but it was only to doze away the time, or else to make the sermon and prayers a mere intellectual exercise. If I drew near to God with my mouth, and honored him with my lips, my heart was still far from him.

Nor did I see any bright prospect. All was becoming gloomy. Life was passing on, and though industriously employed, I had reason to think I enjoyed as much leisure as I could reasonably expect to enjoy at any future period. If my heart was ever to be softened by Divine grace, why not now? If I was ever to be aroused from my stupidity, why not immediately? If I ever intended to set about the work of repentance, why should I longer delay it?—Such thoughts occasionally passed through my mind, but

> "As from the bird the sky no trace retains,
> The parted wave no furrow from the keel,"

so my convictions were evanescent and powerless.

I am not aware that any fear of positive punishment, either here or hereafter, had much weight with me. My distress arose chiefly from the following considerations. The work of redemption had been achieved at an astonishing price; and a world of glory, which I was in danger of losing, laid open to an erring race. Created with faculties which I might bring to the service of God, and endowed with the capacity of *loving* and *enjoying* as well as *approving* EXCELLENCE, I was yet entirely without a relish for this excellence, and daily and hourly growing more and more indifferent, and thus shutting myself more and more effectually out of heaven. Receiving by means of conduct which was morally unexceptionable, the smiles and a measure of the approbation of my fellow men, I felt that I was rapidly hastening to a world where mere morality will only serve as a light to show us the greatness of our eternal loss.

These, so far as I recollect the progress of my

mind, were some of the motives that weighed with me. Positive punishment, I thought, *might* come, but I could not at that time bring myself to fear it, so much as negative misery, or the loss of happiness.*

All this while, I had a few friends who labored with me occasionally, to induce me to seek for Divine aid. Sometimes we sought this aid in company; and I tried to believe the truth of the promise respecting only "two or three" when "gathered together." But all to no purpose. I went on.— How many prayers ascended before the Eternal Throne in my behalf, or whether my friends prayed for me in their closets at all, I have no means of ascertaining. Some of them were men who labored as well as prayed, and prayed as well as labored; and it is highly probable that they were often and earnestly at the mercy seat, on my behalf.

Protracted meetings were occasionally held in the region of country where I resided; and at length one was appointed in the very neighborhood

---

* Perhaps I ought here to say, that the fear of positive punishment has been every day deepening from that time to the present. Perhaps it is owing to the fact, that I every day see it to be more just; and more accordant with a PERFECT CHARACTER in God, as well as with the works of nature.

where I was. I kept about my business. My friends urged me to go to meeting; but I refused. Yet this very refusal led to important reflections; and my conscience was at length roused.

I attended the meeting, but it was as usual, to *hear* and *not* to hear; or rather to hear and not to feel. I saw that a crisis was approaching. I must give up all hope of a cordial reconciliation to God, in the way of the Gospel, and like the devils believe only to tremble; or I must go at once to the Savior. The latter, as I thought, I was unable to do; for there was still much human pride remaining, as was evinced in the desire I felt to do the work myself. There seemed to be some necessary preparation to make, in the first place.

It was resolved, at length, to give up business, give up attendance on public worship, and betake myself to prayer and reflection. Accordingly one morning I shut myself up in my room, determined not to go out of it again till the great point was settled, and I had declared either for God or against him.

Here the ghosts of former skepticism appeared and beset me. What was to be done? Read I could not; prayer was still more impossible. I walked the room. Not a particle of religious sensibility seemed to remain. My heart was like adamant—my affections were riveted to earth and the business of earth, and I could not be disengaged. The more I strove, the tighter it seemed to draw my chains. "Jesus, thou Son of David, have mercy on me," was nearly every thing of prayer I could utter: and this short petition seemed as formal as the language of the proud Pharisee. I almost doubted my own sincerity, even while uttering it.

These thoughts at length struck me: "Why do I not go, at once to the Savior? What am I waiting for? Is he not ready?" Surely, my soul seemed to say, he *must* be. I was musing on this for some time. At last I concluded my difficulties were not immovable, but that there was still a possibility of returning to God.

There was, about this period, another striking change of feeling. From a habit of regarding myself as the centre of the universe, the point on which all my efforts ought to turn, I began to regard GOD as the centre of the moral world. In fact this was a favorite idea or feeling, and one that perpetually recurred; and does to this day.

My condition, in one respect, was now wholly changed. I felt a strong and abiding belief that I should at length be able to yield to and obey Christ. The way seemed plain. It is true, I never felt as if I had already attained; but rather as if I *should*, in the end, repent and exercise that faith, and have right feelings. I could not avoid the conclusion, that God had at length conducted me through the wilderness of error, and given me a sight of the promised land; and I believed, that in his own time I should enter it.

For some months afterward, my friends seemed to have more charity for me than I had for myself. Some of them thought that I had already passed from death unto life. And in the end I adopted the same opinion.

An anecdote may be inserted here, for the benefit of those who undertake to give advice to new converts, especially of ministers. A friend who knew my state requested me a few days after the change of feeling occurred, to call on a distinguished minister in the neighborhood. I did so, and had a full and free conversation with him. On separating, the minister said something not unlike what follows; Well, sir, remember that though I do not say you are a Christian, I advise you to go forward and work out your own salvation with fear and trembling, &c. The expression "I do not say you are a Christian," was uttered in such a tone of voice that I took courage from it; and for some time indulged a degree of hope that the circumstances and state of the case, as I now think, did not at all justify.

But although it should surprise the reader, I must here observe that the idea of uniting with any church hardly occurred for a considerable time; and when it did occur, I rejected it with disdain. So much was I disgusted with such narrow or sectarian measures, as I called them, that it was my intention to stand aloof from any church, or even any sect, as long as I lived. Six or eight months having elapsed, however, I found my views somewhat changed. I found myself united to a church; and going on my way rejoicing, though not without trembling, lest after all I should, as Paul has expressed it, be a *castaway*.

CHAPTER XIX.

CONCLUDING REMARKS.

Present state of the writer.—Appeal to parents.—To the young.—To former disciples.—To associates.

THUS, have I finished my long narrative—my forty year's journey, as it were, in the wilderness. For though the period of my wandering falls a little short of forty years, yet it is sufficiently near that period for the purposes of comparison.

When from Pisgah's top, to which I had climbed to catch a glance at the promised Canaan, I first saw the fair fields which a feeble but kindling faith anticipated as mine; when by rapturous vision, if not Divine guidance, I saw the whole land spread before me from Dan, Naphtali and Gilead on the one hand, to Beersheba, the city of palmtrees, and the land of the Philistines on the other;— when I contrasted the beauty of the prospect before me with the great and terrible wilderness through which God had led me by " a way that I knew not;" how could I help rejoicing in Divine

Goodness, and believing that after such a painful series of wanderings I should know how to prize a better inheritance? What more natural than the conclusion that my estimate of the country into which God was bringing me would always be heightened by a recollection of the troubles through which I had passed, and my many gracious deliverances from peril?

And such was the conclusion I actually made. At first I was almost disposed to bless God that I had been so long placed in the school of error, because I had thereby become not only better disciplined and prepared for the *defence* of the truth, but also better qualified to enjoy it.

But, what a mistake! Not that I cannot, indeed, better sympathize with those of my erring fellow beings—and many such there are—who are treading the same or nearly the same path. Most undoubtedly I can. Each bitter has its sweet. But it costs too much.

But in regard to *actual enjoyment*; if I could speak with a voice that would reach every land which is Christian even in name, I would warn all my fellow men against the delusive and dangerous notion that if they do wander for a little while in error, it is not of much consequence, provided they are not *cut off* in it; since they shall enjoy truth and light the more when they once find it. It is one of the plans of Satan—one of his most successful ones too—to disseminate, far and wide, this delusion, so congenial to the pride and fancied independence and strength of fallen humanity.

Let my fate admonish others to keep close, in early years, to the God of their fathers. Venture not, for one moment, into the path of error. It is but a perplexing, an endless maze, from which if you ever escape, even " so as by fire," you must suffer inevitable loss.

And by *looking at me*, be reminded, once more, of your danger, and of the loss to which you are exposed. Here I stand on the very confines of the land of promise, but am not permitted to go over and take full possession; doubtless, because I am unprepared. The *heavenly* Canaan, I indeed entertain faint hopes of enjoying ; but not the *earthly*. I can climb the mountain's height, now and then, and feast my eyes on the country reserved for others, but I must probably spend my days, at least for ought I see at present, in wandering about these plains ; and in death alone go over to the other side of Jordan. Sometimes I find myself falling back even into the very wilderness from which I have just emerged ; indeed I sometimes stray so far away, that it appears quite doubtful for the moment, whether I ever find my way out again.

Thus I live. I would not for the world go back to Egyptian night and darkness; I am unfit to go forward to the full possession of the promised land. Here I am likely to remain, to make few if any real advances till my last change.

You will say I lack faith; that the promises of God are sure; that it is my own fault if I do not go forward, and enter into full possession immediately. I know the fault is my own. That it is owing to a want of full confidence in God, I also cheerfully concede.

But alas! you know not how I have destroyed myself. You know not how strangely my former skepticism has insinuated itself into all my feelings, and thoughts, and habits. You know not what worlds the devil is permitted to hold out to me; to what an extent he is permitted to assail me; and how feeble my unhappy and unholy habits of thinking render me, in the conflict with him. *Did you know*,—but blessed be God, most of you *do not*, and *cannot* know my condition.*

If my desultory narrative should meet the eye of heads of families, and, in any instance, arrest

---

* See Appendix, note F.

their attention, they will, I trust, permit me to give them a word of exhortation, in this place.

PARENTS! you live in an interesting but critical period of the world's history. Duties devolve on you, more arduous, more responsible, than ever fell to the lot of parents before. Men are every where throwing off what they deem the heavy yoke of authority, both as individuals and as collective bodies. The watch words of the day are *Self-Education*, *Self-Government*, *Free Inquiry*, *Mental Independence*, &c.;—good things enough—but like other good things liable to perversion and abuse, especially in the hands of a race of beings so prone to extremes. Your children catch the spirit which prevails. How can it be otherwise? You may as well expect they can live in the physical atmosphere and not inhale it, as not to inhale the moral atmosphere which is spread around them.

What then will you do? Will you renounce your authority? Because every one claims to be able to act as his own pilot on an unknown coast, will you give up the vessel to him, and let him suffer that shipwreck, which will be almost inevitable? Or will you awake to your condition, and to your increased responsibilities, and do what you can to guide the ship in safety?

Do not suffer yourselves to fall into that delusive error that you must not inculcate your own evangelical religious views on your children while very young, lest you produce a bias in their favor; but that you must leave them to choose their religious sentiments for themselves. The thing is just as impossible as it would be to leave them to form their opinions in their riper years in regard to the kinds of food, or drink they will use. Do what you will, their opinions—their creeds, if you please —on any subject, whether morals, religion, politics, economy or the most common concerns of life, must inevitably be formed. The idea of leaving them on neutral ground, without bias, is all a fallacy; nay, more, it is a " doctrine of devils;" and one of the most popular doctrines the devils ever preached. Be not then deceived by it.

Let those who boast of all the freedom from " sectarianism" and " creeds," as well as all the "charity" and " liberality" under the sun,—let such, I say, bring up their children without prejudice or bias, if they can; but be it yours to train up the child " in the way he should go;" which is " in the nurture and admonition of the Lord."

You will, of course, inculcate the importance, and encourage in him, the practice, as fast as reason is developed, of inquiring and judging for himself, not only whether one thing shall be expunged from his physical creed, and another substituted in its place; but also whether his moral creed shall remain the *same* or not. In other words you will train him to study the word of God, and form opinions for himself. If you have failed, however, to train him up as you ought, you will not attempt to *force* the " tree," now nearly grown, to a direction into which the early " *twig*" might easily have been *guided*, by the gentle hand of parental love.

And if these thoughts have attracted the attention of the young, let me ask their attention for a few moments to one who was once a *child* like them, but who would gladly hope they may escape his errors.

CHILDREN! whether your age be ten, fifteen, or twenty-five, remember that if you still have parents; *you are children*. You know the old maxim, that he alone is fit to command who has learned to obey. Yours it is, then, to obey. Now you are not to acquire the habits of obedience simply that you may know how to command; but because it is your duty to your parents, and well-pleasing to God. If your parents have been successful, they have formed you to habitual obedience so early that you cannot remember when you first learned that disobedience was possible. Habit, early habit, is second nature. Happy, if in you, *obedience* constitutes a *part* of that second nature.

But if you have learned, either earlier or later, that you have *power* to disobey, are you therefore determined to exercise that power? You must naturally expect more or less error in judgment on the part of parents, but let me beg you to *obey* cheerfully and promptly, *whatever may be your age*, unless the command be notoriously unreasonable or unjust; cases of which kind rarely occur.

Above all, hearken to parental *advice*, and like parents themselves, use the reason which God has given you. They bid you *inquire*, on all subjects; but urge you to inquire carefully, and not suffer yourselves to be beguiled by what is specious in appearance, but whose only merit is novelty. You are flattered perhaps by the idea that the past generation took up their opinions upon trust; but that you ought to be wiser, and rise superior to prejudice. Remember, however, that an opinion is not necessarily erroneous *because* it is received upon trust; and that a contrary doctrine is not *true* simply because you *do not* take it upon trust, or because it enables you to stand out of the common ranks of mankind, and to attract the public gaze.

You will hear much said about "fastening your faith on the sleeves of others;" but you may look in vain, the world over, for him who does not receive all his early opinions, on every subject, in this manner. I repeat it, the thing is unavoidable; unless you are brought up—grow up or *vegetate* rather—like Caspar Hauser.

Nay, it is not only unavoidable, but God intended it should be so. It is conformable with the whole course of his dealings with mankind. The conduct which he requires of *his* children, is the surest guide for you in regard to your duty to those who are appointed here below as, in some measure, his substitutes.

God requires of his children obedience, without giving the reasons in every instance; are we therefore to hesitate whether or not we ought to obey?

Doubtless all his commands are reasonable and just; but is it not to be expected that in the present infancy of our existence we may not always be able to perceive their fitness and propriety? Smile you may, at this; but it does appear to me that we are often called to obey both God and our parents, simply because they *command*; when to delay, in order to find out the reason of the command would be perilous.

Independence of opinion, therefore, is not always a virtue; it may in some cases be a vice. To the latest moment of our existence, even in the utmost maturity of intellect, and on the most important subject to which the mind can be called, (I quote the language of Mrs. Fry) " we are not to think for ourselves, that is in all cases, but man is to believe what he is told upon higher authority. And when all human learning shall have enlarged his mind, and heavenly knowledge been added to its stores, and others shall bow before him, as the wisest of men, the greatest grace that can adorn his character, will be at last, as it was at first, to feel that he knows (comparatively) nothing.

" If such be the perfection of Christian character why begin the formation of it in a tone so different? To tell my child, that I, his father, his tutor, appointed by God and man to be his instructor, guide, and governor, am to be judged by his imbecility—that he is to receive no opinion upon my authority—that he is to examine my opinions and judge for himself—that he is not to believe what I tell him, unless I can approve it to his understanding; if I wished to produce in manhood a proud free thinker, or lawless infidel, this is the method I would use—and it would be successful, too;—but not if I desired to see in my child a humble, believing, self-distrusting child of God.

" I speak earnestly on this subject, because I see that very sensible and pious people have, incautiously and without reflection, fallen into this system. It is a bad spirit to cultivate. Disrespect to parental authority is the first evil resulting from it, but it is not the only one ; contempt for all human authority is the next; and in the end, a questioning of the authority of God himself."

I would not have dwelt so long on this subject, my dear young friends, but to warn you to avoid the rock on which I spilt; and, in some respects, split forever. It is true, I may, through infinite mercy in Jesus Christ, be saved at the last; yet if I should be, I can never rise so far in excellence before the Eternal Throne as I might have done, had I attended to my own business, and not aspired to this mental independence of which I have been speaking; but which after all is only a dreamy affair.

Let me urge you, as you value your happiness—your real independence of mind and character,—not to take the first lessons in the *modern school* of "free inquiry." Take one step, and you have no security where your journey will end. It is the way to death and hell. Such I must inevitably have found it, had not Infinite Mercy plucked me " as a brand from the burning."

But if you *will not* hearken to parental caution on this subject, nor to *me*, remember that you were once at least, effectually warned. If you will hearken to the syren song of those who allure you, *go;*—but remember you may never return to your former peace. Go ;—but remember that if you should finally return, it is to mourn while you live, saying ; Alas ! " how have I despised counsel and hated reproof!"

My hand trembles while my conscience assures me that there are one or two more classes of the community whom I ought to address and warn ; First, those friends or disciples whom in one way or another I have misled ;-and secondly, those who have been my associates or accomplices, in this work of misleading others—in what I now regard as neither more nor less than soul murder.— And first, let me address those whom I have misled.

DEAR FRIENDS ; You will remember with what warmth I once entreated you to save yourselves from the erring opinions of the day, and embrace what I regarded as a purer and better system. You will remember, moreover, with what eagerness you listened to my suggestions. Now let me urge you, with equal warmth, if you have not already seen the folly of the way in which I led you, to reflect on the circumstances. Twelve or fifteen years have indeed elapsed since I was with you—conversing, urging, reading with you—and many of our number have gone before us to the world whence there is no return. But you remain behind; and many traces of what passed between us are still impressed on your memories.

Now what was it which most interested you, while I used to complain of the various sects of Christians around us, and especially of the Calvinists, as we called them? Was it not my opposition to what are usually called the doctrines of grace? Was it not that I set myself against total depravity, regeneration, and the doctrines of the cross of Christ, as commonly held, by his followers? Was it the novelty, in any good degree—was it above all the preciousness—of any thing which I taught as peculiar to Unitarianism or any other sect which I then regarded as entertaining improved views? If you examine yourselves to the bottom, I think you will find that it was not what I taught to be true which interested you, but what I taught to be untrue. It was, in one word, my opposition to the humiliating, but most blessed truths of the gospel of our Lord and Savior.

Some of you have been, in the good Providence of God, led back to the truths from which I beguiled you. This I am exceedingly happy to hear. But others, as I have great reason to fear, are yet going on in your sins, less anxious to examine yourselves to see whether you bear the image of Christ, than to find fault with other Christians and other sects, especially with those usually denominated evangelical. In a word, you are still in your sin and selfishness. Be entreated by one who loved you in former times, but who loves you still better now, to embrace Jesus Christ as he is freely offered to you in the gospel; and to believe the doctrines which he taught, whatever they may be. The question, with you, should not be, what is rational, so much as what is scriptural.

God must indeed be a reasonable being, and all his laws must be reasonable laws, whether found in the Bible or out of it. But nothing is more likely than that He who is so infinitely above any of us, in giving laws to us, and especially in revealing to us his character and nature should leave something not fully explained. The wonder with me is, not that there is so much which we are required to believe which we do not fully understand, as that there is so little. The first grand questions are—Is there a God? Has he given laws? and where are those laws to be found? And if we make up our minds that the Bible is the principal or only source of knowledge on this subject; then let us receive what it teaches—whether we understand one-half, two thirds, or the whole of it. If it is the word of God it must, of course, be *rational*.

There is a day coming, when you and I must meet to answer for the manner in which we have treated that which claims to be a revelation of God and his son Jesus Christ. May we never forget it; and what is of more importance still, may we be duly prepared for it!

And now a word or two to my old associates. BRETHREN! We have seen an end if not of "all perfection here below," at least of many of our plans for the advancement of mankind. We have moreover seen an end for this life, of some of our members. One left us from this metropolis; another or two from Connecticut; another from Vermont; another from Kentucky; another from Texas;[*] nor has either of the departed returned to give an account of his reception in the world of spirits.[†] We must follow soon—and according to the views of some of our number, we know not whither.

Now are we sure that there is really so little light shed on the future as we are wont to suppose? Is human knowledge, generally, as limited? Is it really true that man neither knows, nor can know,

---

[*] See Appendix, note G.   [†] See Appendix, note H.

much about his spirituality or his destiny? Is man or is he not, the greatest puzzle in this part of the material universe?

Let me prevail with you on one point, which is that you will let go, for a time, your favorite systems of philosophy, and study the simple and less pretending philosophy of Jesus Christ. No philosophy that I have ever studied, can compare, for one moment, with that. This, I know, some of you admit. You say no book is so precious to you as the Bible; and that since you obtained *new light* it has been ten times more valuable to you than before.

You object that I am narrowed down to a sect; while you have a system of philosophy which embraces all sects. But are you quite sure of this? For my own part, I think there is a little fancy work about this matter, as you view it.

Or if what you say is correct, it does not come well from you. Why object to a single sect, if your views embrace all sects, and are *therefore* meritorious? Is a part objectionable, and is the *whole* desirable? Or is there some crook in your philosophy by means of which you can make the whole to be smaller than a part of that whole?*

Remember, I entreat you, that professing to be

---

* See Appendix, note I.

reasoners you ought to be *good* reasoners. You will not, of course, question the propriety or beauty of shining in our professions. See then, I pray you, that you apply your reason as judiciously to spiritual matters as to temporal ones.

Do not trouble yourselves—as some of you seem inclined to do—about the motives by which I was actuated in coming to my present views and course of conduct. Leave all that to God, and to me. There may have been, by possibility, a mixture of improper motives. It is difficult to know one's self. But suppose there were something wrong taken into the account; does that prevent the consequences of error to you, should it turn out that you have *embraced* error? Will my being a hypocrite, even should I turn out to be one, help you?

It may be an important question with you whether I am right or not; but, it can never be so important to you, as the question whether you are right yourselves. You say much about my being true to my own nature, and you say well; will you not be true to your own? To your own master—not to me, that is primarily or principally—you stand or fall. Is it not so? Must it not be so? Remember too, brethren, that we are growing old. The greater part of our days—should life be protracted, in the case of every one of us who remain, to seventy or eighty years—are spent; and what we do for ourselves or for others, must be done quickly. Exhort one another, says Paul,—and Paul's opinions and advice I know you are accustomed, on the whole to respect—and so much the more as you see the day approaching!

But I must leave you; shall it be forever? You say; "Away with your arrogance—this claiming to be holier than others." But I make no claims of the kind. We certainly shall separate forever, or we shall not. Together we have walked, and held pleasant converse; together we may walk still, while life and breath last—but when they can hold out no longer—what then? This is the question. Shall we part to meet and converse and hold counsel together no more? Or shall we meet again? And if we meet again, under what circumstances?

I am overwhelmed with a mixture of regret, remorse, anxiety and apprehension. I sometimes wish I had not put pen to paper on this subject, but left you, as I am myself left, to the mercy of God. But I am urged to speak—conscience, even—unless I mistake her voice, pleads with me to speak. My heart bleeds for myself—for you—for others. Is it in vain to you—nay worse than in vain? God only knows. To yourselves and to him I leave you. Farewell!

APPENDIX.

Note A. Page 62.

While I am ready to acquit the Unitarians, in general, especially the individual referred to at page 62, of any thing like duplicity, I am equally free to observe that I think they understand, better than most sects among us, the true secret of gaining proselytes to their views; which is by *influence* rather than by anything which carries the appearance of force. They admit and strongly defend the freedom of the human mind.

"There are two principles, says a recent writer,[*] by which men act upon the minds of their fellow men; viz. *power* and *influence*. Power is principally exerted in the shape of authority, and is limited in its sphere of action. Influence has its source in human sympathies, and is as boundless in its operation.

"If there were any doubt which of these principles most contributes to the formation of human character we have only to look around us. We see that power, while it regulates men's actions, cannot reach their opinions. It cannot modify dispositions, or implant sentiments, or alter character. All these things are the work of influence! Men frequently resist power, while they yield to influence and conscious acquiescence."

---

[*] See "Woman's Mission," Chap. I.

Now it has appeared to me, I say, that the Unitarians have been in advance of most other sects, in their knowledge of the power of influence; and hence have taken a more correct way of making converts or proselytes. Not indeed a more rapid way, but one by means of which if these proselytes are once secured, they are usually more effectually secured, and more certainly retained. They seek to *enlighten* mankind, in the first place. Not however—let it be said, once for all—in a proselyting spirit; but because this is the way, in which they are accustomed or trained to make their efforts.

This, as I apprehend, is the secret of their zeal, in this region, in behalf of schools; and in the promotion of certain benevolent objects. When, therefore, I shall say hereafter, that the tendency of elevating our common schools in Boston and elsewhere—that is of rendering them more intellectual than they were before, for this is nearly the sum total of what their friends call elevation—is to promote error of religious opinion, I trust I shall not be supposed to make the charge of malicious intention, or even of a proselytism which is unworthy. I speak only of the tendencies of things; I meddle not with motives; especially the motives of others. Enough for me, if I show that mere intellectual elevation, to the neglect of physical and moral cultivation, tends to Unitarianism, or to what is still worse, without implicating any one in such a design. I know of no plot among the Unitarians or indeed among any other Christian sects, for the secret destruction of those whose happiness its abettors profess to seek.

NOTE B. PAGE 75.

Man is regarded, by the author of this work, as possessing a threefold nature—physical, moral, and intellectual. Now Christianity addresses itself to the *whole being*—is adapted to the wants and development of the whole being. In its application, however, to an individual whose physical nature has been prematurely and excessively developed, it usually makes but little impression. It gives indeed an impulse; but the force does not last long. Where the moral nature has been attended to exclusively, at the expense of the body and the intellectual powers, the result is bigotry and superstition. Where the intellect has been cultivated more than either the physical or the moral part there is apt to be a tendency to speculative views in every thing, but especially in morals and religion. Hence, in part at least, our Universalism, Unitarianism, Rationalism, and in fact our Skepticism. The person whose intellect is excessively developed, while his bodily powers and moral nature have been neglected, is seldom content with the plain simple truths of God's word, but is ever predisposed to modify them, in order to suit them to his own preconceived opinions, and render them more conformable to his own perverted reason. Is it not so? Look abroad among the intellectual men of our metropolis—not among the Unitarians alone and exclusively, but elsewhere—and see if it is not so.

The tendency of civilization has hitherto been to produce an undue development of intellect. Almost all that is called improvement in education contributes to this very result. Men's physical and moral natures are every where neglected; and the consequences are deplorable. Nor is this the worst of it. The evil will increase indefinitely, so long as the present system of education shall continue. Until the body, head and heart can be cultivated harmoniously, Unitarianism must continue to increase. It is not the sending abroad of Agents or Missionaries that can produce very important results to prevent either Unitarianism or Skepticism. Something may indeed be done for the moment, but the effects will not be permanent. When the present generation shall pass away, the millions now in our Infant, Primary, and High Schools will be likely to rise up with their heads filled with all the mysteries of science, but with that neglect of their moral nature and especially of their physical frames, which will produce the most unhappy results. Would we introduce Unitarianism and every species of departure from evangelical truth, into our country, we have but to encourage and extend our present system of intellectual instruction and follow up the common practice of crowding the intellect, and calling it education. We cannot surely be so unobserving as not to see that where this intellectual improvement—of which Germany and England and France and America have been, and still are so proud—has been carried to the highest pitch of perfection, there, and in those countries, cities, and places, evangelical religion has been refined, speculated upon, and subtilised, until it has lost the Spirit of Him who gave it, and become filled with mysticism, rationalism, and every species of error. Would we, on the contrary, promote the spread of truth, pure and undefiled, as it fell from the lips of Him who spake as never *man* spake and led such a life as no man ever yet led, we must attend to *physical, social, and moral education.*

The first years—say till six or eight or perhaps even in some instances ten years of age—must be spent chiefly in the cultivation and improvement of the physical frame and the social and moral affections. Little direct intellectual instruction is admissible in the first years of life, would we form a harmonious and healthful and perfect character. Jesus, the Redeemer of men, set us an example in this respect; from which, however, we have strangely deviated. He was the only instance the world ever saw of a *whole being* in harmony both with the laws of nature and revelation. "The perfect balance of all the intellectual and moral powers" says Miss Jewsbury in her "LETTERS TO THE YOUNG," "was only witnessed in Jesus of Nazareth, and the result was perfection.

No virtue outgrew its fellow; no duty trenched on its opposite, there was a constant parallelism between principles and their application." Nothing can be more just than these remarks; and yet how little do we reflect on this subject—the character and education of the Savior!

How strange it is that while we are constituted with a body and with a social and moral nature, and all this is indispensable to the accomplishment of even the *heavenly* purposes of the Savior, our systems of education should be based upon the principle that every *human* purpose can be accomplished by mere *intellect*.

I repeat it, therefore; until the first years of life are devoted to the cultivation of man, *physically*, *socially*, and *morally*, as well as *intellectually*—and until not only this is done, but the moral and social part and physical frame are allowed to maintain their place, through life, without suffering the intellect even for one hour to gain the ascendency—until this is secured, I say, the current of error must continue to flow, and to swell,—threatening and ultimately accomplishing a degree of moral desolation which cannot at present be measured or estimated.

It has been intimated that there are, at present, increasing facilites in this community, for producing an abundance of what I have called *intellectual monsters*. These facilities consist chiefly in the present character of our schools, to which I have already adverted; and to their agents and instruments.

I have expressed myself so fully on the general intellectual tendency of our schools that I need not enlarge on that point. I will only say more distinctly than I have before done, that the schools of this country are every where exclusively intellectual, about in proportion as Unitarianism and the other usual forms of moral and religious error prevail immediately around them.

224   APPENDIX.

But is not the excellency of the schools of Boston and its vicinity universally conceded? you will perhaps ask. It is indeed; but what then? Does this prove that the public sentiment may not be perverted—and perverted too, in part, by those very schools? It is this perversion of public sentiment of which I complain. The schools could not exist—in their present highly intellectual character—did not the diseased state of public feeling both sustain and demand them.

Some of the agents and instruments of our schools have also a most unhappy tendency. Let me be fully understood on this point. Our schools are suffering, indirectly, from the character of some of the books which have been introduced into them. For it is well known to those who have taken the least trouble to investigate the subject that a considerable proportion of our more popular school books, especially reading books for classes, were prepared by *highly intellectual authors*, and not a few of them by Unitarians. A very large share too, of the more popular juvenile and family books which find their way to the domestic circle, as well as to the school room, originated from the same source.—Nor is it less known, perhaps, that a full proportion of our teachers, especially those who have engaged in teaching within a few years, are either Unitarians, or still worse. Bred in intellectual schools or colleges, but, finding the *professions*, as they are usually denominated, well filled, they have resorted to teaching, or to preparing school books. And, these school books, thus prepared, evangelical christians, almost every where, put into the hands of their children!

I do not say that these books directly teach Unitarianism, or any other form of error; for in general they do not. It is not *because* they directly teach either *moral or religious error* that I complain; but because they DO NOT TEACH EITHER MORAL OR RELIGIOUS TRUTH; especially the latter. They not only exclude every evangelical doctrine, but ALL doctrine. They seem to go upon the principle of keeping every thing of the kind out of sight;—probably in the belief that children should be left entirely at liberty to form their *own* religious opinions unbiassed by the books they read, especially their school books.

Now there is not, under the whole heaven, a more sure, or more effectual way of propagating, or at least of encouraging that indifference to the christian religion, which will induce men to desire a half way house on the road to heaven, than this. And while we are boasting so much that Unitarianism is "on the wane," "getting into its dotage," becoming "gouty and decrepid," &c., may it not be that Unitarians solace themselves with the fact that they have a strong hold upon the rising generation in our schools? May they not well be contented with this; since it needs not a prophet or the son of a prophet to foretell the consequences?—The seed they are thus sowing, through the medium of schools, school books and juvenile books, generally, will spring up in due time, as surely as the laws of the Great Creator continue to operate as they now do; and will as certainly produce a most abundant harvest.

That I am not mistaken, in these views, or if mistaken, am not *wholly* alone, allow me to introduce here an extract from the recent work entitled, "Woman's Mission," written by an English lady, and republished in Boston and New York—in the former with a preface from the Rev. Mr. Gannett, of Boston—himself a Unitarian minister.

"The friends of instruction look upon intellectual culture as the grand panacea for all evils; and the enlightened and benevolent exhaust themselves in efforts to extend to the many the advantages once confined to the few. Good results follow, but not the results expected. Intellectual, by no means involves moral progress—this we see in nations: intellectual, by no means involves moral superiority—this we see, also, in gifted individuals."

The French writer, Aime Martin in his *Sur l'Education des M'eres*, &c., also thus observes:

"It is in vain to seek, in political institutions or intellectual cultivation, the moral regeneration of the world. It is neither industry nor science, nor machinery, nor books, which can make the happiness of a people. All these things are useful in their places, and it ought to be the care of the legislator to multiply them; but if content with having developed the intellect, that earthly part of man, he neglects the soul, that emanation of the Divinity, he will only see around him a multitude, restless, through unbridled passions, tormented by the desire of aggrandizement and the thirst of knowledge. Their instincts, in themselves sublime, become a torment. * * * * All that gives repose to the heart, all that really elevates humanity comes from above. The most intellectual, if they be not at the same time the most religious people, will never be the sovereign people."

Neither of these writers it is true, affirms in so many words, that intellectual without moral improvement renders us actually worse; but may not such a deduction be fairly made from their premises? Does not elevation of the intellect necessarily strengthen the *instincts*, as this writer calls them? And does not the same elevation expose us the more to temptation, at the same time that it does not increase our power to withstand it?

But it may still be asked; What has this to do with our religious opinions? The reply to such an inquiry is easy. Is it not well known and universally conceded that the religious belief of an individual will ever be affected by the state of his heart? Who that feels the workings of depravity within him, and sees clearly the chains that bind him, and yet has not moral energy to resist them, and attempt his freedom, will not be likely to quiet his conscience by a system of religion or of religious views, which softens down depravity, and makes the path to heaven more easy than the Bible does? And will not our children, brought up in the way which excludes the humiliating doctrines of the Gospel from their view, even from their school books, be likely to live and die with very quiet consciences? What but the special grace of God is to hinder it?

Still we need not desire to pull down our schools or destroy our school books. It were better policy, as well as higher wisdom to establish schools and encourage school books of a more elevated character than those which already exist, and which shall be free from the objections and defects to which I have alluded. Especially important is it to improve the family school and purify the church—to reform the one, and evangelize the other. This is the surest way to put down infidelity, as well as to annihilate those forms and systems of education and religion which lead to it.

Note C. Page 100.

Every friend of truth must rejoice that a period has arrived when individuals, among all sects, perceive the utility of friendly discussion and free and impartial inquiry. The word discussion has too long awakened in the minds of men the idea of angry dispute merely; and the words free inquiry that of mere caviling and skepticism. This, however has been an abuse of terms. Rational, friendly discussion has a most important connection with genuine, rational free inquiry; both as cause and effect. Both must be received, or both rejected :—I am for retaining both.

Nor am I willing to concede that Unitarians are the only sect possessing "liberal," "enlarged," or "enlightened views;" or that they are the only people who strive to maintain, inviolably, the "true principles of civil and religious liberty." On the contrary, the great truths of what is commonly called "evangelical religion," are not only consistent with,—but the *almost inevitable result of free inquiry*, and *enlarged and liberal views*.

Free inquiry, in a loose sense of the term, such as is commonly received, *may* lead to evangelical, or to *any other* views, even to skepticism; according to the disposition and propensities of him who indulges in it. But in a more limited and strictly *just* sense, it can never, in my opinion, lead to *any other than evangelical sentiments*.

On this point, I *do* not speak unadvisedly—I *would* not speak uncharitably. It is not a small matter to seem to doubt either the intelligence or the honesty of so large a portion of the human family—for if evangelical views are exclusively accordant with revealed truth, then a considerable number of those even, who profess the Christian name are in a greater or less degree in error,—and not only in error, but inexcusably in it; for there are several sects besides Unitarians, who depart widely from evangelical views, and yet make the highest pretensions to *reason and free inquiry*.

Those who are well acquainted with Unitarianism in this country will be apt to smile at the bustle which this sect is making to devise ways and means to check the progress of skepticism. The danger from it is cheerfully admitted to be as great as they suppose; and I am even willing to admit that the manner in which truth has sometimes been presented by sects orthodox in doctrine, may have had no inconsiderable share in producing the present state of things.

But it is the *remedy* proposed by our Unitarian friends, and not the disease and consequent danger, which unavoidably excites a smile. Can they seriously believe that the views they entertain would, if generally adopted, effect a cure? No doubt they not only *can* but *do* believe it. But it is also believed that they are sadly mistaken.

Suppose they could send forth a troop of missionaries to convert men from skepticism to Unitarianism; suppose, moreover, they could effect their object. What would be gained? How long before these converts would relapse into their former state? At least, what security could be given that a relapse would not be the general result?

In these United States there are two considerable classes of persons to whom the views of Unitarians seem to be peculiarly welcome. Let me be a little more particular with respect to them.

The first class comprises those in whom the nobler intellectual and moral nature has been but feebly developed, while the sensual, or animal part has acquired a strong ascendancy; I mean not those persons alone, who make it the sole purpose of their lives to gratify their animal appetites, but those whose minds are so completely absorbed in the pursuit of wealth, or honor, or pleasure, as to leave no time for attention to the soul; for these persons are so strongly in love with the WORLD, and so utterly destitute of love to the FATHER OF THEIR SPIRITS, that wherever the gospel is preached in its purity, they have usually become disgusted with its strictness. They are ready to listen with attention to views which are less "rigid," as they term them. Represent religion to them as an easy thing—a thing by no means incompatible with much error and self-indulgence;—throw out insinuations against the doctrines they have been accustomed to hear; tell them about the dignity of their nature, and how this nature has been hitherto abused; complain first cautiously, and afterwards more boldly of the conduct, and even of the intentions of ministers and professors of religion;—and above all, take pains to appropriate to yourself or to your sect the title of "*liberal,*" "*charitable,*" &c., and you have their ears and their applause; I had almost said their *hearts*.

Again, just throw out a severe remark on some of the peculiar doctrines of orthodoxy, rather, I might have said, of the Bible, such as man's depravity, his need of regeneration, eternal punishment, the decrees of God, or the nature of Christ,—and you will find these people gather round you at once. I have delivered many a Unitarian discourse to a large audience of this description, and with great apparent success.* Had it not been for my success in this way and the reflections to which it led, I might at this moment have been a thorough-going Unitarian.

A person of ingenuity, especially if he were not a minister, might go through the "length and breadth" of this land of "steady habits," and through the *steadiest* parts of it too, and collect in every place, either from taverns, tippling houses, lottery offices, theatres, or gambling houses,—nay, even from not a few of the debating societies which exist—associations of Unitarians, who would promise well at first, and from some of which churches might finally be gathered.

In order to this, however, the aid of another—a second —class of the community is indispensable; and the facilities which now exist, and which are destined to exist, ere long to a greater extent, for obtaining it, afford the principal reason why I think Unitarianism has not reached its zenith. I allude to our intellectual, speculative, superficial men. The absolute amount of intellect possessed is not essential in constituting an "intellectual" person; it is only the *comparative* amount;—the predominance of mere intellect, over both the animal and moral nature. As in the case of those of whom I have just been speaking, the animal nature is developed at the expense of head and heart, especially the

---

* I do not mean sermonizing; but rather discoursing before a circle or a club. I have never sustained the ministerial office.

APPENDIX. 231

latter, so that the individual might be regarded as possessing a *body* merely, i. e., is a physical monster; so in the case of those to whom I now refer; the intellectual nature is developed at the expense of every thing else; and this constitutes a being with a *head* merely; *another* form of monster.

These two classes of men are the principal persons who become infidels or skeptics in our country. They first imbibe prejudices against evengelical doctrine—partly because it strikes at the root of error, even at the native depravity of the heart and its utter disrelish for holiness—and partly because it is often unfaithfully or injudiciously presented to them in the language and lives of its ministers and professors. Thus they reject one doctrine and another, and another; becoming like Priestly, first Unitarians (though they may not know that the name would properly apply to them) then the better sort of Deists or Rationalists,—and, lastly skeptics. Sometimes the tracts these various sorts or sects of men distribute assist them in their progress downward,—and sometimes they pursue their career without their aid.

From these two classes of men, then, come the skeptics, i. e., from the two extremes of society. They are usually the *scum* and the *dregs*. A few, indeed, of the middling class,—the plain, the honest, the sensible and the moral,—may fall in with them, but not generally. It is he that "doeth evil," that "hateth the light" of truth. What motives has the moral and peaceable citizen to cavil at rigid views in religion, as they are sometimes called? On the subject of decrees he will generally answer the cavils of his neighbors, in language like the following. "There are no decrees that hinder a man from doing as he pleases; nor are we taught that there are." Similar common sense replies are as readily given on other subjects.

Note D. Page 167.

Let me be understood on this point. I do not mean to intimate a doubt that there are any truly evangelical people among the Unitarians; for I know there are some such. Perhaps, indeed, I was a little unfortunate in my first acquaintance. But I do mean to say that their evangelical character, however excellent, and their piety, however intense, cannot be the fruit of their doctrines, but must be the result of better views; views, I mean, more in accordance with fact and the Bible. Such persons are pious in spite of their Unitarianism, and not as the consequence of it.

Grant indeed, what is most certainly true, that there is every grade of belief among our friends the Unitarians,—from an almost orthodoxy to the rankest Socinianism, or Humanitarianism; still they who come the nearest to orthodoxy, are far from being Trinitarians. "Make the Savior any thing you please but Deity," says one of their most distinguished writers; "but make him not equal to the Father." There is, and must be, forever, a dividing line between us. It does not mend the matter to say that some who belong to orthodox churches, entertain the same views of the Savior; we know this is so. Our present Unitarians, many of them, were once members of orthodox churches; they did not change their denominative position, till sometime after they had changed their sentiments. Especially is this true of the older people among them.

One of the Unitarian ministers of Massachusetts, once advised me, when I was about renouncing the views to which he was attached, to read the "Natural History of Enthusiasm." Circumstances prevented me from complying with his request, which I exceedingly regret. Yet the author of the same work, in his "Spiritual Christianity," more recently from the press, has the following remarks, which considering that he warmly disclaims all sect, are certainly worthy of attention.

"If therefore it were asked; Is a trinitarian faith of much importance to practical piety? we should be content to say—trace the history either of individuals or of churches that have renounced it, and you will find an answer. A trinitarian faith, clear of every evasion, and excluding even the disposition to look for evasions, we hold to be the basis of all christian piety."

"It is when christianity, is spiritually understood, and when whatever tends to substitute symbols for realities is rejected, that a trinitarian faith is brought to bear, with effect, upon the understanding, the heart and the life. If this faith be doubtfully or distrustingly held, is it any wonder that it is found to be ineffective? or if it be held in conjunction with notions that either oppress the heart, or which favor the propensity to rest in formalities, then ought we to suppose it can exhibit its proper influence?—But we are speaking of a spiritual and cordial trinitarian faith; and then we affirm it to be the basis of the only virtue which deserves the name,—a serious, reverential, happy and affectionate devotion of the whole nature to God the Father, the Son, and the Holy Spirit."

Note E.   Page 177.

I have always regretted, when I have read the suggestion of Payson, that he should have thrown out such an idea as that to which I have referred on page 177, without explaining himself. For my own part I am quite ready and willing to present the grounds of this momentary skepticism.

It always arises—I believe in every instance—from a conviction of the greatness of the change, physical, intellectual, social and moral, which Christianity promises to man, while so few of its followers appear to take any hold on these promises. Can it be, I say to myself, that people really believe in such things as sin, holiness, sanctification and heaven? For if they did, is it possible they would live as they now do? Can a system be true which has been in the world eighteen hundred years, and yet has produced so little effect?

Yet there is another side to the subject; and the thoughts of what Christianity *has really done* immediately rush in, and dispel the dark cloud which was coming over. Besides, I cannot help thinking it to be no mean proof of the truth of Christianity, that despite of the wickedness which I know to be in the human heart, and the evidence with which the earth is filled, it should have survived as long as it has. Must not a religion, I say again, to myself, which has outlived the storms of eighteen hundred years, and even gathered strength amid every attack—must not such a religion be divine? Must it not indeed, as its Divine Author has affirmed, be built upon a rock?

I know not how it may be with other minds of a different structure from my own; but to me the consideration that Christianity has not been wrecked long ago in the mighty ocean of depravity, by the storms, national and individual, which have assailed it, is an internal evidence of its truth, quite as overwhelming as the consideration of its having actually accomplished so little.

One thing more still. The seed of truth is sown, and has germinated. Its roots, in fact, are beginning to take hold on the soil in which it is imbedded. Now in the vegetable world —to carry on the analogy—we can judge something of what will be the whole existence, to say nothing of size, of a tree or shrub, by the time taken up in coming to maturity.

In proportion to its slowness of growth will be the strength and duration of its manhood, and indeed of every subsequent period of its existence. It is even so to some extent, with animals and men, and strikingly so with aggregates of men— I mean nations. Why should we not carry these analogies to Christianity? I have said that Christianity has taken root. What if the process has occupied eighteen hundred years? Is not this very slow growth in its favor? May we not hope for a manhood, glorious and enduring, in the same proportion?

Note F. Page 204.

The thoughts and feelings expressed at page 204 are those which too often prevail; and which at the time the text was written, now several years ago, truly represented the habitual condition of the soul. Nevertheless it is but justice to myself, and above all, to the cause of truth which I hold dear, to say that I have one evidence of progress in the heavenly road; viz: a deep and abiding and increasing sense of the exceeding sinfulness of sin.

When I first began to see things as I trust they really are, it was not so much the sinfulness of sin, or its punishment which distressed me, as the thought of the loss of happiness or heaven to which I was exposing myself. This fact, however, I have more than alluded to already. But within a few years past I have found the miseries of sin and its present and future punishment more and more distressing to me.

Perhaps indeed I have been led to this by the peculiar nature and character of my religious studies. A part of my time for three or four years past has been spent in maturing a series of essays—lectures rather—on the ten commandments. In pursuance of this task I have found the law of

God, as David found it, exceeding "broad :" and have been led to those views of the exceeding sinfulness of sin, and withal of my own sinfulness, which might once have overwhelmed me and driven me to positive despair, but which now have no such effect. The more I see of the extent and enormity of transgression against the holy law of God, natural and revealed—nay, even of my own transgression—the more does it lead me to magnify the plan of salvation through Jesus Christ; to rejoice in the hope that I am interested in it, and to go forward from conquering to conquer.

And herein I confess, with cheerfulness, and with gratitude to Almighty God my heavenly Father, is the occasion, at times of taking a little courage. For perplexed though I am, I am not as I trust wholly forsaken; cast down though I am, not wholly destroyed. I deem it something—perhaps a matter of encouragement—that I am permitted to see more and more how weak and unwise and guilty before God I am, and yet the sight does not produce, of late, any feelings of despondence; but only urges me onward to the battle.

All this may seem gratuitous; yet the exceeding darkness of the picture presented at page 204 seemed to require that something of the kind should be said, though it were at the risk of being misunderstood or even misrepresented.

Note G.   Page 215.

A brief account of these deceased associates may not be wholly without interest.

The first to whom I have referred was a physician; and in the main, a most excellent man. Towards the close of his life, however, his mental faculties became somewhat disordered; and it was under the influence of the hallucination that he was most distinguished for his "liberalism." He died as he lived.

There were two more from Connecticut. One of these was a young man—intelligent, but somewhat vicious; as his whole course of life plainly indicated. I always had hope of him, however, while he lived, that his morals would improve. How was it possible, I said, that one who talks so much like a good man, should long retain so many bad habits? But he, too, died as he lived; and died suddenly and unexpectedly.

The other was a man who was somewhat advanced in years when I first became associated with him. For a time I thought him virtuous, and this was his general reputation. He was grave, and therefore, as it was thought, *wise;* just and inoffensive to others; and therefore, it was supposed, *good.*

How much in raptures would he be, at times, at the "great truths" of Channing and Dewey! And what high hopes he had of the future! I always observed, however, that he held his property very closely; and that he was no friend to self-denial, in any of its forms.

Not long after I was led by Divine Providence to evangelical sentiments, I called on this man and tried to undo the mischief I had done him. But I found him deaf to the voice of reason. He was becoming intemperate, decidedly so; and so were his wife and some of his children. And he was not only intemperate but though between fifty and sixty years of age, grossly and openly licentious. He, too, died as he had lived, only rather worse. He died a victim to his open and horrible transgressions of both the natural and moral laws of God; and without any marks of penitence. For several years before he died, I wrote him occasionally, forewarning him of his end; but it appeared to do no good. Or if any convictions of sin were induced, they had the fate of the morning dew—to pass quickly away.

The individual in Vermont, was a man of much literary merit, and, I have no doubt, a searcher after truth. Yet he began the search, as I think, with a wrong principle. He began by *assuming the position* that he ought to believe nothing but what he knew certainly; and that he knew but a few things with certainty—such as could be proved from the testimony of the senses. Strange that a man who would *assume* nothing and *take for granted* nothing, should begin by assuming a principle which was to say the least a very doubtful one. Such, however, is human inconsistency.

He was a moral man, and probably died as he lived; but of this I cannot speak with certainty. He died quite young—scarcely thirty years of age.

My associate who died in Kentucky was in the main an excellent man; but of a highly speculative turn of mind, and exceeding worldly and ambitious withal. Much as he loved his family and friends, he would traverse sea and land, year after year, and encounter every form of peril, to provide for the future—for himself and a large family—when the present had the strongest claims for both. He was a man in middle life; and much beloved, except by his religious friends and neighbors, who always—and justly—regarded him as skeptical. He was seized with a fever, suddenly, and died in a state of delirium—far from home and from relatives and friends. *He* died, no doubt, as he lived.

The last to whom I shall refer here, has been mentioned at page 57. My prediction concerning this young man, made long before his death, was too painfully verified. Forgetting every god but money, he pursued his profession—for he was a physician—in various parts of the South-west, with almost entire indifference to the state of his mind and heart. He died suddenly two or three years ago, at Houston in Texas. Of the manner of his death I have heard nothing; but I do not believe I hazard any thing in saying that he died as he lived.

It will be seen that not all of these individuals were immoral men; just as it is with the survivors. Dr. Chalmers speaks of a world of atheists as tolerable for a time, and so might a world of skeptics be tolerable for a time, especially *in the midst of a world of Christians.* It is difficult to see the narrowness and nakedness of skepticism, in a community where the general state of the public sentiment has been moulded by Christianity.

Note H. Page 215.

I have alluded to the instance that none of my deceased accomplices have returned from the other world to give the survivors information. The fact is that one of our number— one whom I have mentioned in Note G—promised another of the fraternity, that if he should die before *he* did, and if there was a possibility of return, he would appear to him after his death and give him information concerning the future state. It is perhaps needless or almost needless to add that he has never yet made his appearance; and that his comrade has given up the hope of seeing him this side of the grave.

Note I. Page 132.

My friends, some of them—my former friends I mean—talk a great deal about my losing my individuality; merging myself in a sect; being untrue to myself, &c. But because I am attached to a sect, am I therefore sectarian in my feelings? And cannot a person attach himself to others in any sense on any circumstances, without losing his individuality? Those very individuals who complain of me, attach themselves to their own families. Are they not afraid of losing their individuality by the attachment? To carry out their "idea" to the full extent, ought they to marry? Nay, more; ought they to belong to civilized society, or especially to obey its laws?*— May I not throw back the charges they make, upon themselves?

The greatest freedom which can be enjoyed, in this world, is that freedom wherewith Christ makes his followers, if true followers, free; and shall the servant of Christ be charged with narrowing himself down—making a slave of himself—by belonging to the church of Christ? Who like the true christian, preserves unimpaired his own individuality of character? Who, like him, is so truly independent? Who, like him, is true to himself, to his own idea, to his own nature, &c.

Never, in my life, did I feel so truly free to examine all things, prove all things and hold fast that which is good, as at the present moment. If my attachment to a sect has in any degree abridged my rights or impaired or diminished my freedom, I am certainly ignorant of it. Nor do admit a believer, as some of my liberal brethren seem to think necessary, that the views I now entertain—the general doctrines I mean of evangelical people—are in all respects so far accordant with truth as to be susceptible of no alteration or improvement. I believe great discoveries remain to be made, of Bible truth; and I trust in God I shall ever hold myself open to conviction of the truth from whatever quarter it may come, and whether or not it may accord with my former or present sentiments. "To the laws and to the testimony."

---

* Some of them in fact—true to their *ideas*—are already beginning to doubt on this very point of obedience to the laws of human governments. Doubts respecting matrimonial obligation will soon follow of course.

Gould, Kendall, & Lincoln's Publications.

THE FOUR GOSPELS;
WITH NOTES,
CHIEFLY EXPLANATORY;
INTENDED PRINCIPALLY FOR
Sabbath School Teachers and Bible Classes,
AND AS
AN AID TO FAMILY INSTRUCTION.
BY HENRY J. RIPLEY,
Prof. of Bib. Lit. and Interpretation in Newton Theol. Inst.

STEREOTYPED EDITION.

This work should be in the hands of every student of the Bible; especially every Sabbath school and Bible class teacher. It is prepared with special reference to this class of persons, and contains a mass of just the kind of information wanted. It also contains a splendid colored Map of Canaan.

RECOMMENDATIONS.

The commendatory notices received by the publishers have been so numerous, that they are enabled to give but short extracts from a few, which will enable the reader to form an opinion of the merits of this work.

The undersigned, having examined Professor Ripley's Notes on the Gospels, can recommend them with confidence to all who need such helps in the study of the sacred Scriptures. Those passages which all can understand are left " without note or comment," and the principal labor is devoted to the explanation of such parts as need to be explained and rescued from the perversions of errorists, both the ignorant and the learned. The practical suggestions at the close of each chapter, are not the least valuable portion of the work. Most cordially, for the sake of truth and righteousness, do we wish for these Notes a wide circulation.
BARON STOW,   R. H. NEALE,
DANIEL SHARP,   J. W. PARKER.

[From R. E. Pattison, D. D., President of Waterville College.]

I should sooner recommend the Notes to that class of persons for whom they were designed, than any other with which I am acquainted.   R. E. PATTISON.

[From Rev. S. Chapin, D. D., Pres. of Columbia College, Washington, D. C.]

One excellence of Professor Ripley is, that he helps the reader where he needs help, and when he does not, he lets him go alone. On plain texts, his notes are not obtruded; but on the obscure, they are sound and satisfactory. In a word, I view the work as possessed of much merit, and well adapted to promote biblical knowledge and the cause of religion.   S. CHAPIN.

Gould, Kendall, and Lincoln's Publications.

[From Rev. Luther Crawford, Sec. Am. Bap. Home Miss. Society, N. York.]

I cannot but regard this as the *safest* and *most unexceptionable* work there is to be found of the kind, and should rejoice to hear of its extensive circulation through all our families and Sabbath schools. LUTHER CRAWFORD.

[From Rev. J. S. Bacon, Lynn, Mass.]

The notes are almost wholly explanatory; they are brief, to the point, and are for the most part confined to those passages which, to the young and inexperienced especially, really need some explanation. J. S. BACON.

[From Rev. R. Turnbull, Pastor of the South Baptist Church, Hartford, Conn.]

I have had a fair opportunity of becoming acquainted with the merits of the work. I can unhesitatingly say, that it is almost every thing I could wish as a class-book.
ROBERT TURNBULL.

[From Rev. J. A. Warne, Editor of the Comprehensive Commentary.]

His criticisms are just, judicious, and unostentatious; and often the results of much research. It may not seem proper to institute comparisons between Ripley and Barnes; and yet I will just say, that Professor Ripley is, in my judgment, by far the safer, the more modest, and the less ostentatious guide; and I cannot but wish he were adopted *universally*, in place of Barnes, in our Sabbath schools. JOSEPH A. WARNE.

[From Rev. N. Kendrick, D. D., Prof. in the Hamilton Lit. and Theol. Inst.]

I think them superior, for the use of Sabbath schools, to any exposition I have seen of this part of the divine Word. The correctness of sentiment which they inculcate — the judgment with which the most important points of the passages are selected for explanation — the perspicuity and precision with which these are treated — the judicious references to ancient usages, which throw light on difficult texts — their adaptation to awaken in youth an interest for the study of the sacred Scriptures, and to aid their inquiries after divine truth — give them a decided claim upon the patronage of the Christian community. NATHANIEL KENDRICK.

[From Rev. B. T. Welch, D. D., Pastor of Pearl St. Church, Albany, N. Y.]

The notes, though brief, contain much information of an important character, and are, in my judgment, admirably adapted to the object for which they were written. B. T. WELCH.

[From Rev. Jeremiah Chaplin, D. D., late President of Waterville College.]

He seems to have hit on the proper medium between that conciseness which leaves the mind of the reader unsatisfied, and that prolixity which exhausts his patience and loads his memory with useless lumber. This is a rare excellence in writings of any kind, and especially in those whose object is to illustrate the Word of God. JEREMIAH CHAPLIN.

Gould, Kendall, & Lincoln's Publications.

MALCOM'S TRAVELS.

TRAVELS IN SOUTH-EASTERN ASIA; embracing Hindustan, Malaya, Siam, and China; with Notices of numerous Missionary Stations, and a full Account of the Burman Empire; with Dissertations, Tables, &c. By HOWARD MALCOM. In two volumes, 12mo.; with a superb original Map of South-eastern Asia, five Steel Plate Engravings, and about seventy Wood Cuts.

CHARACTERISTICS OF THE WORK.

It is not a mere diary of events which befell the traveller, but contains thousands of facts, dates, numbers, prices, &c. &c., which are either original, or gleaned from sources not accessible in this country.

Incidents, anecdotes, and scenes, have been freely introduced; but only such as tend to make the reader better acquainted with the country.

The most perfect impartiality is shown to every sect of Christians, and such details given of the various missions as make the work equally acceptable to every persuasion.

Such sketches are given of the history of the countries, towns, and missions which are described, as serve to throw light upon their present condition.

The map is beautifully executed, and may be considered original. Many important corrections have been made by actual observation, and the remainder is chiefly drawn from original and unpublished surveys by British officers, engineers, and surveyors, to which the author was politely granted access.

The pictures are wholly new, and form an important addition to our oriental illustrations. No pains or expense has been spared in these or the mechanical execution. Five of these are on steel, showing landscapes of Maulmain, Tavoy, Mergui, and Sagaing, and a curious page, exhibiting specimens of 16 different oriental languages.

A great part of the work relates to countries almost entirely unknown, even to the best informed persons in our country.

The author, from the important character of his mission, his intercourse with distinguished civilians and experienced missionaries, his deliberate stay at each place, his previous familiarity with foreign countries, and his long experience in the Board of Missions, enjoyed the highest advantages for gathering ample and correct details for the work.

Chapters on the mode of conducting modern missions, or on the measure of success which has attended the enterprise; on the almost unknown tribes in and around Burmah; and on other important subjects, are added at the close of the work, and constitute no small part of its value.

The work has received the highest commendation from the press; and the best proof of the estimation in which it is regarded, is in the unexampled sale of the work. Near FOUR THOUSAND copies were sold within one year from its first appearance. In its mechanical execution it surpasses any similar work ever attempted in this country.

Gould, Kendall, & Lincoln's Publications.

THE ORIGIN AND HISTORY OF MISSIONS; a Record of the Voyages, Travels, Labors, and Successes of the various Missionaries, who have been sent forth by Protestant Societies and Churches to evangelize the Heathen; compiled from authentic Documents; forming a complete MISSIONARY REPOSITORY; illustrated by numerous Engravings, from original Drawings made expressly for this Work. By the Rev. JOHN O. CHOULES, New Bedford, Mass., and the Rev. THOMAS SMITH, late Minister of Trinity Chapel, London. Fifth Edition, continued to the present time.

The original cost of the stereotype plates, engravings, &c., to this work, considerably exceeded $7000, which necessarily so enhanced the price of former editions ($13 per copy), that many were precluded from purchasing it, who would otherwise have gladly done so.

The present proprietors, having purchased the work at a considerable deduction from cost, and being desirous of placing it within the reach of *every one* wishing to possess this valuable repository of missionary intelligence, have determined to put it at the *very low price* of $7 per copy, trusting that by this means it will receive from an enlightened Christian community the *extensive patronage* which the merits and importance of the work demand.

RECOMMENDATIONS.

The plan and object of the ORIGIN AND HISTORY OF MISSIONS having been submitted to us, we beg leave most cordially to recommend it to the attention of the religious public, considering it highly calculated to extend the interest which is already felt on behalf of the great missionary enterprise.

Rev. RUFUS ANDERSON, D. D., } *Secretaries of the American*
Rev. DAVID GREENE, } *Board of Commissioners for Foreign Missions.*

Rev. LUCIUS BOLLES, D. D., *Corresponding Secretary of the Baptist Board of Foreign Missions.*

Rev. P. VAN PELT, JR., *Secretary of the Protestant Episcopal Missionary Society.*

Rev. WILBUR FISKE, D. D., *President of the Wesleyan University, Middletown, Conn.*

Rev. FRANCIS WAYLAND, D. D., *President of Brown University.*

[Extract from the report of the Committee of the Baptist General Convention on Publications.]

THE ORIGIN AND HISTORY OF MISSIONS, by the Rev. J. O. Choules, having been referred to the notice of this Committee, they have fully examined the number already printed, and possessed themselves of the views of the conductors of the work. The Committee are happy to express their entire confidence in the qualifications of the author, and belief that the work will richly merit the attention of the religious public.

Gould, Kendall, & Lincoln's Publications.

GESENIUS' HEBREW GRAMMAR; translated from the Eleventh German Edition. By T. J. CONANT, Professor of Hebrew and of Biblical Criticism and Interpretation in the Theological Institution at Hamilton, N. Y. *With a Course of Exercises in Hebrew Grammar, and a Hebrew Chrestomathy, prepared by the Translator.* 2d Edition.

This work has been but a short time before the public, but has met with much favor. It was immediately adopted into Harvard University, Newton Theological Institution, Hamilton Institution, Washington College, &c.

NOTICES OF THE PRESS.

The work of Gesenius requires no eulogy from us; nor is this the place to enter into a detailed examination of his theoretical views or practical exposition of the structure of the language; but we concur with the translator in considering that, as a philosophical arrangement and explanation of its grammatical phenomena, it has no equal; and that it is particularly distinguished by a chaste simplicity, and attractive clearness of method, — qualities which not only imply a correct taste and logical understanding, but evince, also, a thorough mastery of the subject. Professor Conant has rendered a substantial service to the cause of Biblical learning, and done honor to the important denomination of which he is a member. Besides executing with excellent fidelity and good judgment his translation of the Grammar of the great Hebraist of the age, he has some useful additions of his own, and has, in numerous instances, corrected mistakes of a too common class, which, if they give little trouble to some readers, are the worst annoyance to others, — that of errors in reference. He has also made additions of a very judicious as well as moral character, in a series of grammatical Exercises. The typographical execution is in the best style of the Cambridge University printers. The letter-press is beautiful, and all but immaculate." — *North American Review.*

[From the Boston Recorder.]

Professor Conant has executed his task with great ability. He does not appear merely in the character of a translator; the Chrestomathy and Exercises prepared by him form a very valuable addition to the work. The latter, especially, are prepared with great skill and ability, in such a way as to lead the student forward step by step, making him thoroughly familiar with each point as he advances.

One other point of extreme importance in such a work, we must not fail to notice — the correctness of printing. This is truly wonderful. And when we add that the typography — at least the English part of it — is as beautiful as it is correct, we have perhaps said as much as is necessary to recommend the book to all students of the Hebrew.

Gould, Kendall, & Lincoln's Publications.

DR. HARRIS'S WORKS.

THE GREAT TEACHER. Characteristics of our Lord's Ministry. By the Rev. JOHN HARRIS, D. D., of Epsom, England. With an Introductory Essay, by HEMAN HUMPHREY, D. D., President of Amherst College.

MAMMON; (Prize Essay;) or, Covetousness the Sin of the Christian Church.

UNION; or, The Divided Church made One.

ZEBULON; (Prize Essay;) or, The Moral Claims of Seamen stated and enforced. American Edition, edited by the Rev. WILLIAM M. ROGERS and Rev. D. M. LORD, Boston.

THE WITNESSING CHURCH. "Ye are my witnesses, saith the Lord, that I am God."

THE HOUSE OF PRAYER. "My house shall be called a house of prayer for all people."

Probably no writer of modern times has so much engaged the public mind as Dr. Harris. All his works have been favorably received, extensively reviewed, and both the style and spirit highly commended. The following extract from a review of "The Great Teacher," may justly be applied to the style and spirit of all his writings:—

"The book itself must have cost much meditation, much communion on the bosom of Jesus, and much prayer. Its style is like the country which gave it birth — beautiful, varied, finished, and every where delightful. An American writer on the same subject, would have more resembled his own country — rising now and then, again descending to the valley. But the English writers carry you on — like their own M'Adamized roads — safely, rapidly, delighted, and unfatigued. But the style of this work is its smallest excellence. It will be read. It ought to be read. It will find its way to many parlors, and add to the comforts of many a happy fireside. The reader will rise from each chapter, not able, perhaps, to carry with him many striking remarks or apparent paradoxes; but he will have a sweet impression made upon his soul, like that which soft and touching music makes when every thing about it is appropriate. The writer pours forth a clear and beautiful light, like that of the evening light-house, when it sheds its rays upon the sleeping waters, and covers them with a surface of gold. We can have no sympathy with a heart which yields not to impressions delicate and holy, which the perusal of this work will naturally make."

Gould, Kendall, & Lincoln's Publications.

New and Improved Edition.
MEMOIR OF GEORGE DANA BOARDMAN,
LATE MISSIONARY TO BURMAH,
CONTAINING MUCH INTELLIGENCE RELATIVE TO THE BURMAN MISSION.

BY REV. ALONZO KING, of NORTHBORO', MASS.

A correct likeness of Mr. Boardman, engraved on steel, from a painting in possession of the family, and a beautiful vignette representing the baptismal scene just before his death, have been added.

[From Rev. J. O. Choules, of New Bedford.]

I have read the Memoir of Boardman with great satisfaction. * * * The great charm in the character of Mr. Boardman was his fervent piety; and his biographer has succeeded admirably in holding him up to the Christian world as the pious student, the faithful minister, and the self-denying, laborious missionary. To the student, to the Christian minister, it will be a valuable book, and no Christian can peruse it without advantage. I hope our ministering brethren will aid in the circulation of the Memoir. Every church will be benefited by its diffusion among its members. Yours, &c., JOHN O. CHOULES.

[From the Christian Watchman.]

This Memoir belongs to that small class of books, which may be read with interest and profit by every one. It comprises so much of interesting history; so much of simple and pathetic narrative, so true to nature; and so much of correct moral and religious sentiment, that it cannot fail to interest persons of all ages and of every variety of taste.

[From Rev Baron Stow.]

No one can read the Memoir of Boardman, without feeling that the religion of Christ is suited to purify the affections, exalt the purposes, and give energy to the character. Mr. Boardman was a man of rare excellence, and his biographer, by a just exhibition of that excellence, has rendered an important service, not only to the cause of Christian missions, but to the interests of personal godliness.

Yours, with esteem, BARON STOW.

Gould, Kendall, & Lincoln's Publications.

MEMOIR OF MRS. ANN H. JUDSON,

LATE MISSIONARY TO BURMAH.

New and Enlarged Edition.

Including a History of the American Baptist Mission in the Burman Empire to the present Time.

BY JAMES D. KNOWLES,

Professor of Pastoral Duties in the Newton Theological Institution.

EMBELLISHED WITH ENGRAVINGS.

Twenty-five thousand copies of this work have been sold in the United States, besides several editions in England. It has also been printed in French, and is about to be published in the German language; which shows that it is a work of no *ordinary* interest.

[Extract from Mrs. Hale's Ladies' Magazine.]

We are glad to announce this work to our readers. The character of Mrs. Judson is an honor to American ladies. The ardent faith that incited her to engage in an enterprise so full of perils; the fortitude she exhibited under trials which it seems almost incredible a delicate woman could have surmounted; her griefs, and the hopes that supported her, should be read in her own expressive language. Her talents were unquestionably of a high order; but the predominant quality of her mind was its energy. The work contains, besides the life of Mrs. Judson, a History of the Burman Mission, with a sketch of the Geography, &c., of that country, and a Map accompanying, and a beautifully engraved portrait of Mrs. Judson.

[From the London New Baptist Miscellany.]

This is one of the most interesting pieces of female biography which has ever come under our notice. No quotation, which our limits allow, would do justice to the facts, and we must therefore refer our readers to the volume itself. It ought to be immediately added to every family library.

Gould, Kendall, & Lincoln's Publications.

MEMOIR OF REV. WILLIAM CAREY, D. D., forty Years Missionary in India. By Rev. EUSTACE CAREY. With an Introductory Essay, by FRANCIS WAYLAND, D. D., President of Brown University. With a correct Likeness.

[From the Monthly Paper of the Baptist General Tract Society.]

This is a work of surpassing interest, which no Christian can read without profit. The mechanical execution is excellent, and reflects much credit on the enterprising publishers. They have given to the American public an imperishable work, that will be perused with intense interest by generations yet unborn. We have seldom, if ever, read a book which has impressed us with such a conviction of the importance of its being most extensively circulated. With the Memoir of our own Mrs. Judson, it ought to have a place in every family and in every library.

[From the Boston Recorder.]

A Memoir of Dr. Carey must of necessity give an account of the rise of Baptist Missions in the East Indies, their embarrassments, their struggles, and their success. For this reason, as well as on account of the character of Dr. Carey, it must be a work of intense interest.

[From Zion's Herald.]

The compiler observes in his Preface, that his endeavor has been to exhibit the Christian and the missionary, rather than the scholar. We think he has succeeded. It is in the character of a Christian missionary that Dr. Carey preëminently shines. It was through his labors, under the blessing of God, that a character and stability were given to missionary operations in India, which have justly made them the admiration of the Christian world. We compliment the publishers for the beautiful style in which they have issued this book.

[From the Richmond Religious Herald.]

The name of Carey awakens feelings of the most interesting character in the mind of every reflecting Christian, whose heart is alive to the prosperity of the Redeemer's kingdom on earth, and who longs for the spiritual welfare of a perishing world. The life of the founder of modern missions, the pioneer in those efforts which, we believe, are destined to fill the whole earth with the glory of God, and to cause the kingdoms of the earth to become the kingdoms of the Lord, cannot be perused with ordinary emotions, nor without feelings of devout gratitude, that God was pleased, in his own time, to raise up an instrument so well qualified for the mighty undertaking.

Gould, Kendall, & Lincoln's Publications.

PECK'S NEW GUIDE FOR EMIGRANTS TO THE WEST; containing Sketches of Ohio, Indiana, Illinois, Missouri, Michigan, &c. &c. By J. M. PECK, A. M., of Rock Spring, Illinois. *Second Edition.*

CAMPBELL AND FENELON ON ELOQUENCE; comprising Campbell's Lectures on Systematic Theology and Pulpit Eloquence, and Fenelon's Dialogues on Eloquence. Edited by Prof. RIPLEY, of Newton Theol. Inst.

AN EXAMINATION OF STUART'S ESSAY ON BAPTISM. By HENRY J. RIPLEY, Prof. Biblical Literature at Newton Theol. Institution.

FULLER'S DIALOGUES ON COMMUNION. Second Edition.

THE THEATRE, in its Influence upon Literature, Morals, and Religion. By Rev. R. TURNBULL. Second Edition.

JEWETT ON BAPTISM. The Mode and Subjects of Baptism. By MILO P. JEWETT, A. M. Second Edition.

EIGHT VIEWS OF BAPTISM; being a Review of "The Baptized Child." By Rev. WILLIAM HAGUE.

MORRIS'S MEMOIRS OF FULLER. The Life and Character of Rev. ANDREW FULLER. Edited by RUFUS BABCOCK, JR., D. D.

MEMOIR OF ROGER WILLIAMS, the Founder of the State of Rhode Island. By JAMES D. KNOWLES, A. M.

MEMOIR OF REV. WILLIAM STAUGHTON, D. D. By Rev. W. S. LYND, A. M. With a Likeness.

LIFE OF PHILIP MELANCTHON; comprising an Account of the most important Transactions of the Reformation. By F. A. Cox, D. D., LL. D., of London. From the Second London Edition, with important Alterations by the Author, for this Edition.

MEMOIRS OF HOWARD THE PHILANTHROPIST; compiled from his Diary, his confidential Letters, and other authentic Documents. With a Likeness and Vignette.

TRAVELS OF TRUE GODLINESS. By the Rev. BENJAMIN KEACH, London; and a Memoir of his Life, by HOWARD MALCOM.

BEAUTIES OF COLLYER. Selections from Theological Lectures by Rev. W. B. COLLYER, D. D., F. S. A. With a fine Engraving.

IMITATION OF CHRIST. By THOMAS A KEMPIS. A new and improved Edition, edited by H. MALCOM, A. M. With Engravings.

CHURCH MEMBER'S GUIDE. By J. A. JAMES, A. M., of Birmingham, England. Edited by J. O. CHOULES, A. M. A new Edition, with an Introductory Essay, by Rev. HUBBARD WINSLOW, Boston.

FEMALE SCRIPTURE BIOGRAPHY, including an Essay on what Christianity has done for Women. By F. A. Cox, D. D., LL. D., of London. Two Volumes, with four Engravings.

SAINTS' EVERLASTING REST. By RICHARD BAXTER. Abridged by B. FAWCETT, A. M.

HELP TO ZION'S TRAVELLERS. By Rev. ROBERT HALL. With a Preface, by Dr. RYLAND. Edited by Rev. J. A. WARNE.

SCRIPTURE NATURAL HISTORY; containing a descriptive Account of Quadrupeds, Birds, Fishes, Insects, Reptiles, Serpents, Plants, Trees, Minerals, Gems, and Precious Stones, mentioned in the Bible. By WILLIAM CARPENTER, London. With Improvements by Rev. GORHAM D. ABBOTT. Illustrated by numerous Engravings, also Sketches of Palestine.

WINCHELL'S WATTS, enlarged, being an Arrangement of all the Psalms and Hymns of Dr. Watts. With a Supplement.

THE SACRED MINSTREL; a Collection of Church Music, consisting of Psalm and Hymn Tunes, Anthems, Sentences, Chants, &c., selected from the most popular Productions of nearly one hundred different Authors in this and other Countries. By N. D. GOULD.

Check Out More Titles From HardPress Classics Series In this collection we are offering thousands of classic and hard to find books. This series spans a vast array of subjects – so you are bound to find something of interest to enjoy reading and learning about.

Subjects:
Architecture
Art
Biography & Autobiography
Body, Mind &Spirit
Children & Young Adult
Dramas
Education
Fiction
History
Language Arts & Disciplines
Law
Literary Collections
Music
Poetry
Psychology
Science
…and many more.

Visit us at www.hardpress.net

Im The Story
personalised classic books

"Beautiful gift, lovely finish. My Niece loves it, so precious!"

Helen R Brumfieldon

★★★★★

UNIQUE GIFT

FOR KIDS, PARTNERS AND FRIENDS

Timeless books such as:

Kids

Alice in Wonderland • The Jungle Book • The Wonderful Wizard of Oz
Peter and Wendy • Robin Hood • The Prince and The Pauper
The Railway Children • Treasure Island • A Christmas Carol

Adults

Romeo and Juliet • Dracula

- **Highly** Customisable
- **Change** Books Title
- **Replace** characters names with yours
- **Upload** a photo (on inside page)
- **Add** Inscriptions

Visit
Im The Story.com
and order yours today!

CPSIA information can be obtained
at www.ICGtesting.com
Printed in the USA
BVHW091859220819
556561BV00021B/5108/P